P9-CRO-512

Raising the Curve

Most Berkley Books are available at special quantity discounts for bulk purchases for sales promotions, premiums, fund-raising, or educational use. Special books, or book excerpts, can also be created to fit specific needs.

For details, write: Special Markets, The Berkley Publishing Group, 375 Hudson Street, New York, New York 10014.

Raising the Curve

*A Year Inside
One of America's 45,000*
Failing Public Schools*

RON BERLER

BERKLEY BOOKS, NEW YORK

THE BERKLEY PUBLISHING GROUP
Published by the Penguin Group
Penguin Group (USA) Inc.
375 Hudson Street, New York, New York 10014, USA

USA / Canada / UK / Ireland / Australia / New Zealand / India / South Africa / China

Penguin Books Ltd., Registered Offices: 80 Strand, London WC2R 0RL, England
For more information about the Penguin Group, visit penguin.com.

This book is an original publication of The Berkley Publishing Group.

RAISING THE CURVE

Copyright © 2013 by Ron Berler.
All rights reserved. No part of this book may be reproduced, scanned, or distributed in any printed or electronic form without permission. Please do not participate in or encourage piracy of copyrighted materials in violation of the author's rights. Purchase only authorized editions.

BERKLEY® is a registered trademark of Penguin Group (USA) Inc.
The "B" design is a trademark of Penguin Group (USA) Inc.

Berkley hardcover ISBN: 978-0-425-25268-0

An application to register this book for cataloging has been submitted to the Library of Congress.

FIRST EDITION: March 2013

PRINTED IN THE UNITED STATES OF AMERICA

10 9 8 7 6 5 4 3 2 1

Cover photos: school backpack on hook © Fuse / Getty Images; classroom © Fumie Kobayashi / Getty Images.
Cover design by Danielle Abbiate.
Interior text design by Tiffany Estreicher.

The publisher does not have any control over and does not assume any responsibility for author or third-party websites or their content.

This book describes the real experiences of real people. A few names and identifying characteristics have been changed and in one instance a composite character has been used to protect the privacy of the individuals involved, but none of these changes has affected the truthfulness and accuracy of the author's story.

Penguin is committed to publishing works of quality and integrity.
In that spirit, we are proud to offer this book to our readers;
however, the story, the experiences, and the words
are the author's alone.

For Carol, my loving, lovely wife

Prologue

February 2010

The Brookside Elementary School gymnasium in Norwalk, Connecticut, was rocking. You could feel the infectious dance beat—*Chocka-boom-boom. Chocka-boom-boom-bomp*—as it pulsed from a boom box the size of a microwave oven. The sound reverberated out the gym door, past the far ends of the main hallway, down the classroom corridors. In the main office, the two secretaries looked up and sashayed in their chairs. The speech pathologist fought a losing battle to hold the attention of an autistic third grader. In the cafeteria, a custodian sweeping up from lunch pushed his broom to the beat.

A party atmosphere filled the air. The celebrants—nearly two hundred high-chattering third, fourth, and fifth graders—milled about the floor. Some sang along to the music; others danced in place. Cliques of children shrieked to one another above the din.

Around the edges of the cinder-block room stood the principal, the assistant principal, and nine teachers, tasked with keeping things in line.

The adults didn't want to interfere. This was Friday afternoon, the last school day in February. When the children returned from the weekend, they'd walk into a changed academic world. For the next nine school days, they'd spend part of each morning taking a forty-five-minute or one-hour segment of the Connecticut Mastery Test (the CMT), the annual, state-mandated, standardized test on reading, writing, and math skills for all third, fourth, and fifth graders that served as Connecticut's exam for No Child Left Behind (NCLB).

The students—about 20 percent of them white, roughly 15 percent African American, the rest Hispanic, almost 60 percent sufficiently impoverished to qualify for free or reduced-fee lunches—had been preparing for these exams for nine weeks, since the day they returned from Christmas break. Their teachers had altered the curriculum, cutting back on science, history, and social studies—which the CMT did not test—to focus on the three Rs. The exams assessed exclusively reading, writing, and math.

The faculty and administrators hoped their students would score well. They were far from confident. Brookside was not exactly the Harvard of Norwalk, and Norwalk, a struggling, diverse city of eighty-four thousand ringed by four of metropolitan New York's toniest suburbs, was hardly the Harvard of Connecticut. At the time, all nineteen of its public schools were failing, and Brookside, a pre-kindergarten to grade five school, had one of the poorest records of all. Since the signing of No Child Left Behind into law in January 2002, Brookside had amassed a perfect record of failure, 0 for NCLB.

The streak had been threatened just once. In 2007–08, the school had come within a single student of the roughly 79 percent required that year for passing in language arts and 82 percent for math, but the next year had fallen back. In 2008–09, its third graders slipped to second to last in the city in reading, and tied for second to last in math. Its fourth graders finished last in writing and second to last in reading. The fifth graders fared better, but only slightly. A second consecutive poor showing could expose the school to dire consequences—not the students but the faculty and administrators. David Hay, the principal, worried that parents would pull their children from Brookside, costing the school, potentially, as much as $25,000 in lost federal transportation funds. There was precedence for worse; the state had taken over operation of Hartford's failing public school district in 1997. Jobs could be in jeopardy. So Mr. Hay had decided to throw a pep rally for the students taking the 2009–10 exams, in hope of pumping them up with sufficient confidence to believe they could succeed.

A new song blared from the boom box: "The Cha Cha Slide," by Mr. C the Slide Man. The dancing started up again—boys solo, girls in pairs, mimicking the intricate steps they learned watching music videos. Several waved homemade posters made that morning in class, the kind you see when the TV camera pans the student section at a college basketball game. You Are Ready. You Can Do It, read one. Don't Give Up, exhorted another. Mrs. Magrath's fourth graders raised the blue-and-white pompoms they made in class and led a CMT locomotion cheer.

At last, Mr. Hay stepped to the apron of the stage and signaled for the music to stop. The teachers hushed their students, motioned them to sit on the floor. Mr. Hay smiled, trying to convey optimism.

"You've been working hard," the principal began. He looked upon the sea of hyped-up, anxious children and paused ever so slightly. He had intended to charge them up with a spirited pep talk. But something in their expressions, he said later, made him change his tone. The students had been under inordinate pressure the last nine weeks, preparing for the exams. What they needed most, he decided, was a gentle hand. "I expect just one thing from you," he told them, quietly. "That you do your best. Keep trying. Don't give up." He softened his voice even more. "Remember, no matter what you do, your family will still love you, and we'll still love you. You won't be forgotten."

Linda Schaefer, the school's literacy specialist, took the stage next. Since the beginning of the school year, she had worked long hours with individual students on their reading and writing skills and with teachers on classroom strategies for imparting those skills. Though she possessed impeccable credentials and talent, much seemed on the line for her program. The previous June, she had lost her part-time literacy instructor due to a school board–mandated budget cut. That part-time position had been a full-time one until it had fallen to a budget tightening the year before. Additional cuts that coming June seemed likely. Mrs. Schaefer wasn't a classroom teacher; potentially, her own position was vulnerable. She was understandably anxious that the students improve their scores. So perhaps she didn't read in their faces what Mr. Hay had. "I know it may not seem like your score matters," she said with urgency, "but every one of your scores counts. You have to say, 'The CMT is important to me, it's important to Brookside School.'"

The softer mood Mr. Hay had sought vanished. Some teachers, picking up on Mrs. Schaefer's theme, began a rhythmic handclap. The students joined in, many of them stamping their feet. Miss Sutton signaled her third grade class to stand and chant a poem they'd written that morning:

CMT's in the atmosphere.
We're not afraid,
We're not afraid.
We will rock the CMT this year.

Mr. Morey's fifth-grade class rose next and shouted in unison: "We're all in this together! We're all in this together! We're all in this together!"

Each of the school's third-, fourth-, and fifth-grade classes (nine total) took their turn with a chant or cheer. By the time Mr. Hay retook the stage, the kids were revved up as if on a sugar high. Small wonder. Along the gym wall to the side of the stage, a group of teachers distributed squares from a vanilla sheet cake with chocolate icing. There was no calming the children now. Mr. Hay, fighting for their attention, pointed to the confetti of pastel-colored paper slips that covered the gym floor behind them. "I want each of you to pick up a piece, read it, and remember it," he said. The kids scrambled after them as if they were candy. Don't Give Up, read one. Always Do Your Best, urged another. I Can Do It, encouraged a third.

The music started up again, another high-energy hip-hop song: Samantha Jade's "Step Up," from the popular 2006 teen film of the same name. This time the volume was at full blast. The movie tells the story of a child from the wrong side of the tracks with one chance to "step up" and fulfill his dreams. It's questionable whether the Brookside kids connected the song to their uphill battle to pass the CMT, but Mr. Beckley, the third-grade teacher in charge of the music, did. The children danced till the final bell rang, danced down the main corridor to their lockers, where they grabbed their books and coats, and paraded out the front entrance, where their school buses waited. Few understood that the scores would never show up on their report cards, that the CMT graded the school and its staff, not them. "All we can do now is hope," Mr. Hay said, as he watched the students leave.

The CMT came and went. The teachers returned to the district's standard curriculum for the last three months of the school year. For the fifth graders, that meant, in addition to the three Rs, learning about the life cycle of a flower, the Boston Tea Party, and how a legislative bill is proposed and passed. In mid-June, the school term ended. Nearly a month went by before the standardized test scores arrived.

The scores, while not good, were better than the results from the previous year. Brookside had advanced from last among Norwalk's twelve elementary schools to third to last—still far from passing. On the bright side, achievement rose high enough to save Brookside from being classified a school "in need of improvement" and thus open to severe, corrective measures. It made "safe harbor," a classification for failing schools whose scores nonetheless have leaped 10 percent or more. "Of course, improving ten percent isn't all that hard when you start from where we started," Mr. Hay said, in his office that summer. "Next year, the passing grade for the CMT jumps another ten percent [to about 89 percent of students achieving proficiency], and from there the number keeps getting higher. By 2014, all our students are required to be proficient. We'll have about as much chance of passing then as when we started."

Not everyone in Norwalk that summer was as willing to accept the U.S. Department of Education's judgment about Brookside and the city's public schools in general. Mayor Richard Moccia was adamant. "How can you say our schools are failing," he asked, "when you look at what our students have accomplished, from science competitions to the arts? How can you say that when you look at our dedicated teachers and staff, when you look at our improving scores?" Mayor Moccia noted the revitalized, downtown waterfront nightlife district known as SoNo; the Maritime Center, with its first-class aquarium and IMAX theater; the high-tech, hands-on Stepping Stones Museum for Children. "This is not a failing city," he insisted. Audra Good, Brookside's Parent Teacher Organization (PTO) president, felt the same. "All three of my children have gone to Brookside," she said. "Two are still here. I work in the school as a teaching assistant. I'm here every day. I love the school. It's not failing, to me. I think it's a wonderful place to learn." Mr. Hay didn't believe Brookside was failing, either. "I don't pay that much attention to CMT scores," he said. "It's no secret we're struggling. I'm more interested that we keep making progress, that our scores keep improving, that we keep raising the bar for our students."

Nevertheless, Mr. Hay was in his office, at his computer the day the test scores were released in July, crunching numbers, analyzing the results in a dozen different ways. By grade, by race, by income, by subject matter, by comparison to other elementary schools in Norwalk, by comparison to elementary schools statewide.

The test results colored everything. Henceforth, Mr. Hay had already decided, his teachers would spend more time on vocabulary and less on spelling, because the CMT did not grade spelling. That the fourth graders, for the purposes of the exam, needed to know only their multiplication tables for two, five, and ten. That the fifth-grade teachers needn't panic when their students handed in an awkward or grammatically challenged piece of writing because the CMT merely tested their ability to read a short, fiction or nonfiction passage and deliver a passable summary.

Mr. Hay spent the morning jotting notes to himself, knowing that among the brotherhood of public school principals, he was hardly alone. (Forty-five miles away, on the eve of his 2011 retirement after serving seven-plus years as principal of Manhattan's perpetually failing High School of Graphic Communication Arts, Jerod Resnick remarked, "A hundred ninety-nine New York City principals wish they were me.") That July, Brookside was one of 19 public schools in Norwalk, 281 schools in Connecticut and 28,000 in the United States judged as failing. The total would soon grow far worse. The following March, U.S. Secretary of Education Arne Duncan would tell legislators at a House Education and the Workforce Committee hearing that by the end of the 2011–12 school year, 82 percent of all U.S. public schools could be failing.

That's a crazy number, one that begs the question: Just what is a failing school?

Chapter 1

September 2010

Marbella didn't have any choice. Much as she didn't want to, she had to get moving. Outside her bedroom door, she could hear the bustle of wake-up activity. Her three older sisters were already padding about, getting ready for the first day of school. Downstairs, she could hear the refrigerator opening, the clatter of silverware on the kitchen table. Her mother was fixing cheese-and-ham omelets for breakfast. Her father, who owned a small but successful landscaping business, was long gone.

Rubbing her eyes, the slender, dark-haired ten-year-old made her way to the bathroom. She couldn't help but stare at an enormous poster of Justin Bieber taped to her sister Melanie's bedroom door. Both Marbella and eleven-year-old Melanie had a serious thing for the teen singer, whom Marbella referred to as "my love."

Marbella's own room was filled with Bieber posters, CDs, dolls, and fan magazines.

She pulled on a short-sleeve top and shorts—the day promised to be a scorcher; sunny, reaching ninety-three. On her way downstairs she glanced at the tiny alcove snuggled between the banister and a window overlooking the street. A week earlier a potted plant had sat at its center. Now it was pushed to one side. A white work desk and matching chair now occupied the space. The desk set was brand-new. Her mom and dad had placed it in the alcove, thinking Marbella would be better able to concentrate on her homework there. Last year, in fourth grade, she'd done her studying at the kitchen table amid a hubbub of barking dogs, chatty sisters, and Mom preparing dinner. At the moment, the desk was empty, save for a pair of decorative pen and pencil buckets and some knick-knacks arranged on shelves mounted on the rear of the desk. Soon—perhaps that very afternoon—it would be crowded with homework and books.

Marbella liked the look of her new workspace, if not its function. She wasn't the world's most dedicated student. Fourth grade had been a poor year academically for her. She'd begun the school term reading as an entry-level third grader, and had progressed very little. Her problems had run the gamut, from fluency—the ability to read with pace, pronunciation and consistency—to comprehension. Part of the trouble had been her class. Six children, including two rambunctious boys—Chandler and Carlos—had proved expert at pushing their teacher's buttons. The teacher had been relatively inexperienced. When discipline had broken down—and it had broken down often that year—Marbella and her two best friends, Hydea (pronounced Hi-*dee*-ah) and Aajah (pronounced like *Asia*), had been quick to pile on. In that classroom, you really had had to stay focused if you wanted to learn. That had been the other part of Marbella's problem: She hadn't seemed convinced of the importance of school.

Around Marbella's house, her take on education was a minority view. Her parents—naturalized citizens, her mother a Colombian, her father a Panamanian who emigrated to the United States in the 1980s—hoped all four of their daughters would attend college. Melka, nineteen, their oldest, was already enrolled at the local community college. Maryrose, fifteen, and Melanie, both dedicated students, were expected to follow. Mom, who had dropped out of school in the ninth grade to give birth to Melka, had since returned to class to earn her high school degree.

All worried about Marbella. According to Melanie, the only consistent way to get her to do homework—even housework—was to bribe her. Marbella's standard fee for household chores such as washing the dishes, sweeping the kitchen, or cleaning the downstairs bathroom was an ice cream. For those, Dad paid. But he was rarely home when Marbella returned from school. In his absence, Melanie, studious and hardworking, felt obligated to step in. "If Marbella didn't want to do her homework and just wanted to go straight out and play, I would tell her, 'Do your homework and I will give you a dollar,'" she said. "I had a little box full of dollars and I would give her one." Marbella might not give her best effort, but at least she would complete her assignments.

That morning, Marbella climbed into her mom's SUV and headed to Brookside, less than a mile away, on an uncertain note. She had hoped to be assigned to Mrs. Keefe's fifth-grade class. Mrs. Keefe had a reputation for handing out cookies and candies and for throwing lots of parties. Both Melanie and Maryrose had had her, and each spoke of how much fun Mrs. Keefe had been. Marbella's mother could have requested Mrs. Keefe for her youngest daughter but didn't think it necessary. "I just figured she had my other girls, so Marbella would have her, too," she said. Instead, Mr. Hay had assigned her to Mr. Morey's room, in an effort to control her behavior. Mr. Morey was six feet three and had a deep voice. Marbella had never had a male teacher before, and she wondered what he would be like. Tough, probably. On the bright side, Hydea and Aajah were in her class again, as were Chandler and Carlos.

A cross the street from Marbella and twelve houses down, Hydea was antsy to get going. She didn't need anyone to wake her up for the first day of school. Still, the tall, lanky ten-year-old African American couldn't believe the summer was already over. To Hydea, it seemed like fourth grade had never ended. For the second straight year, she'd been forced to attend summer school. Her teacher had told her it was to improve her reading. Hydea knew she was behind. So did her grandma, a retired insurance clerk who worked for years in the Norwalk Public Schools central office. They just didn't realize by how much.

According to Mrs. Schaefer, the literacy specialist, midway through fourth grade, Hydea was reading several steps below Marbella, at a low third-grade level. But her case was a little different. Hydea tried hard. Too often, though, she just didn't get it. She'd read a paragraph and struggle to explain it orally. Marshaling her thoughts on paper was even more challenging. Still, while Hydea's fluency was below average, it wasn't low enough to place her on Mrs. Schaefer's watch list. For a while the girl had sneaked by. But as fourth grade had progressed and discipline in her classroom fractured, Hydea had started fooling around, and her effort had declined. At that point her teacher had recommended her for summer school and Mrs. Schaefer had become involved. "I had to test any student going to summer school," Mrs. Schaefer said. "That was when I really took a look at her." She was shocked by the result. The girl had regressed to reading at a high second-grade level.

That July Hydea had paid the price. Every weekday morning for a month, she had reported to Jefferson Science Magnet School, another school in the district, where she had plowed through a long fiction book—she couldn't recall the title or make much sense of the plot. And now it was time to start fifth grade. It seemed to her she'd had almost no vacation.

Hydea rolled out of bed and placed Snuggles, the stuffed, red bear with whom she sleeps, atop a shelf, where it shared space with two other stuffed bears, a Bible, a music box, and a stuffed monkey named Jizzle. The cuddly, red bear was a long-ago gift from her late mom, who'd suffered from a congenital heart condition and had died from complications after undergoing surgery, when Hydea was three and a half years old. Back then, she and her mom and dad had lived in Atlanta. Hydea still wasn't sure why she'd moved to Norwalk shortly after, to live with her grandma, her seventeen-year-old half-sister, Billi, and her twenty-one-year-old half-brother, Shane. At first she had felt so untethered, she had barely talked with her siblings. Now Grandma's five-room rental apartment, located on the first floor of a subdivided, single-family home across the street from a pizza parlor and two doors from a church social center, was home.

Hydea dressed and shuffled past her homework desk—a faded piece of furniture opposite Billi's. Upon it was a tape dispenser, ruler, stapler, an adding machine, and a jar of green-stemmed, ballpoint pens that bloomed at their ends into exotic, plastic flowers. Framed citations attesting to her participation in the district's annual science fair hung like diplomas on the wall. To the right was a fishnet sack filled with books, including *Junie B. Jones and Her Big Fat Mouth*, the grade-three-level title she was currently reading. To the left was a flat-screen TV that she and Billi shared. The TV, and a computer crammed in a nook in the front hallway, got a lot more use than the books. Over the summer, Hydea briefly had grown excited about reading and had registered for her first library card. "Grandma took me and said to the librarian, 'We're looking for some books for my granddaughter.' And then she took us upstairs and through a door where there were lots of books," Hydea said. But after a second visit, she stopped going. She couldn't really explain why. "I guess I mostly like to play," she said.

Hydea had mixed feelings about returning to school. She wasn't looking forward to another year of reading and math—another subject that gave her trouble. But she was excited she'd been assigned to Mr. Morey. Her friend Chandler knew lots of graduating fifth graders, and all had reported that the tall, athletic teacher was nice and didn't give much homework. She walked to the sidewalk to catch her school bus.

By the time the two friends arrived at Brookside, just after nine A.M., the walkway leading to the school—a sprawling, red-brick, ranch-style building with a playful, blue trim—brimmed with children. They spilled from yellow school buses and family cars, backpacks slung over their shoulders, loud, jostling one another, carefree and oblivious to the troubles their school faced, even apart from the CMT.

Since the previous spring, rumors had abounded that, after seven years at Brookside, Mr. Hay would soon be leaving. He and his wife had placed their Norwalk house on the market. The couple's son had died, and they'd decided to return to north-central Massachusetts—where they'd both been raised and educated, and where he had taught in and administered elementary schools for thirty-four years, the last eight as a principal—to be closer to family. Mrs. Hay was already back in Fitchburg, Massachusetts, decorating their new home. The faculty and staff were unsettled. Mr. Hay, sixty-three, tall, gray haired, rumpled, and a little paunchy, was a skilled, extraordinarily popular administrator. The veteran fifth-grade teacher Mrs. Bohrer, for one, had already hinted that if and when Mr. Hay left, so would she.

The staff knew he had rented a Spartan, four-room apartment on the second floor of what once was a single-family home on a busy Norwalk street. It was in line, actually, with how many of his students lived. Mr. Hay had furnished it with a bed, a kitchen table and chairs, a twenty-five-inch TV, and a large coat rack on which he hung the bulk of his clothes. "One room is bare," he said, in his broad Massachusetts accent. "I don't even use it." He didn't socialize much; he felt it inappropriate to mix too closely with his faculty. He spent most nights alone, watching televised sports or reading biographies. Once a month, perhaps, his land-lord, Mrs. Magrath, the Brookside fourth-grade teacher, invited him to dinner.

The rumors didn't dissipate, even after Mr. Hay assured the staff he was staying. Truth is, he planned to remain at Brookside another three years, in part because he loved his job but primarily to qualify for a ten-year Connecticut state pension, in addition to one he'd already earned from Massachusetts. His deal with Mrs. Hay was simple. Every Friday after school let out, he climbed in his silver Hummer and drove the three hours to Fitchburg, ar-riving, he hoped, before the start of that night's Red Sox telecast. Sunday evenings he returned to Norwalk.

Weeknights, without much to occupy him, Mr. Hay immersed himself in the school and in strategies for its improvement. The last couple of days he'd felt unsettled; he had too many things on his mind. Brookside's operating budget, for one. In June, the local board of education had pared $1.4 million from the district's over-all, $151.1 million budget from the previous year, costing Brook-side one teaching position and, worse, a part-time literacy coach. The school's CMT language arts scores were already deficient, and the previous year's fifth graders, the school's top-performing class, had departed for middle school. As if that weren't enough, the state-mandated proficiency rate had increased 10 percent this year, to about 89 percent. "There's no way we're going to pass," he said one morning in his office, matter-of-factly.

Money issues hindered Brookside in ways both big and small. Mr. Hay lacked the funds to replace the computer room's twenty-three, eight-year-old HP 8000 Elite laptops, all of which were painfully slow, and almost all of which were missing one or more keys. Nor did he have the means to send the school librarian on a book-buying spree to the biannual Scholastic Book Fair at the company's Danbury, Connecticut, warehouse, as he had in the past. To top it off, in June the school board had hired a new superintendent, and Mr. Hay knew that probably meant a coming, radical change in curricula.

That morning, he drove to school early. He wandered the corridors, perusing the teachers' new wall displays, then repaired to his office to answer e-mails. Upon finishing, he searched the Internet for math and science educational websites his faculty might find useful. It had gotten to the point at which it was almost a hobby. When he found a website he liked, he sent a mass e-mail to his faculty with the link. A few teachers used them. Most, he suspected, deposited them in a file and never looked at them again. He shrugged. "You try," he said.

There was one other critical problem the school faced. Though Mrs. Schaefer hadn't told anyone, she had decided to retire at the end of the school year. It wasn't a decision she'd made lightly. The pressures on her literacy program had mounted as funding continued to shrink, and the sixty-three-year-old could feel herself wearing down. Over the last few years, a series of school board budget cuts had reduced her department from two full-time specialists to one full-timer and one half-timer, to now having to service Brookside on her own. It was an impossible task, one that made little sense given the districtwide imperative to improve reading and writing. Scores had continued to improve despite the cuts, but only to a point. Nearly a quarter of Brookside's students lacked the reading skills to achieve proficiency on the CMT, and more than half failed to reach the more stringent level the Connecticut State

Department of Education established as the state goal. One third fell short of the state benchmark for writing skills as well. Teachers struggling with slow readers would stop Mrs. Schaefer in the hallway and ask what the school board members could be thinking, cutting back on the one staff position that could most impact students' reading and writing scores. The literacy specialist shrugged. She had no answer.

Many faculty members arrived extra early the first day of school, but Mrs. Schaefer saw no need. She wouldn't be seeing students just yet. Over the summer her job description had changed, for the third time in three years. Instead of concentrating on individual children, her new mandate was to train the faculty on how best to teach reading, comprehension skills, and writing to the kindergartners, first graders, and second graders—the most critical learning years for the school's emerging readers. It was an excellent idea. Together, a staff of trained educators could reach many more students than she ever could, working alone. But how long would this program remain in place? The choice was not hers. Title I of the No Child Left Behind Act, which provides supplemental, federal funding to help schools in impoverished districts achieve their academic goals, paid half of Mrs. Schaefer's salary, which entitled the U.S. Department of Education to define the thrust of her program. It was the only way Mr. Hay could afford her. The problem was, there was no consistency to it. One year, her mission was to work with kindergarten to second-grade readers. The next, to focus on remedial readers; the following year, mentoring teachers. It made long-term planning impossible.

Mrs. Schaefer knew one thing for certain. Regardless of the Department of Education's desires, come January 2, the first school day after Christmas break, and for the following nine weeks (more than 22 percent of the school year), she would have to limit her work with the younger students and their teachers, and concentrate on the third, fourth, and fifth graders in preparation for the March CMT. "The lower grades don't take the CMT," she explained.

For all Mr. Hay's talk of being less concerned with Brookside passing the exams than his students making steady progress, he still felt considerable pressure from the superintendent and the school board to achieve. His sense of urgency filtered down to the staff. And so, after the school's abysmal 2008–09 CMT showing, he adopted a fresh tactic, one that some teachers grumbled about, but ultimately accepted. His faculty would teach to the test, particularly during the nine weeks leading up the CMT, with history, civics, and science taking a backseat. When the children studied math, they'd work not from their regular, *Growing with Mathematics* text, but from an official CMT study guide. When they studied reading, comprehension, and writing, the same protocol would apply.

Mrs. Schaefer was one of the grumblers. "We're not teaching them literature," she complained of the reading passages in the study guides. "We're teaching them to think and write to a template." But Mrs. Schaefer was a good soldier; she had worked at Brookside since 1988, twenty-two years, and she deeply wanted the school to succeed. Two years earlier, when Brookside had come within a single student of passing the CMT, Mrs. Schaefer had approached Mr. Hay with an unusual idea. What if she ran an in-school tutoring program for students on the cusp of grade-level proficiency in reading and writing? "One student!" Mrs. Schaefer had exclaimed. If she could work every day with eighteen border-line students, she said, six each from grades three, four, and five—children who, with a daily extra half hour of scaffolding, might have the potential to pass—maybe it would carry the school over the top. Mr. Hay was all for it. Mrs. Schaefer spent much of that fall reviewing student histories, consulting classroom teachers, and making character judgments. The students she selected that year were not entirely sure why they were being pulled from class every day. Some tried hard with Mrs. Schaefer, others did not. A handful reached proficiency on the exam, but not enough to affect Brookside's overall score. Still, it was a start. She had repeated the program the following year, and this school term would do so again. Already, she had begun the process of identifying her new candidates.

Mrs. Schaefer was standing outside her office that first school morning, helping direct traffic down one of the main hallways, when Marbella and her circle of girlfriends passed on an intersecting corridor, en route to Mr. Morey's class. Marbella was too involved in conversation to notice her.

Marbella. Mrs. Schaefer had worked with her before, in a small group in third grade and individually in second grade. Marbella could act silly at times. She didn't always give her best effort. "Working with a student like that," Mrs. Schaefer said, shaking her head, "is really a waste of my time." But there was no denying Marbella's potential for reaching proficiency. She'd have to think about her. About Hydea, too. Mrs. Schaefer was intrigued by Hydea. She didn't think Hydea's fourth-grade teacher had been particularly skilled. Mr. Morey, she thought, might bring out the best in the girl. Mrs. Schaefer considered her a real possibility.

The children snaked down the gray-and-blue-flecked linoleum hallway, past the cafeteria and gymnasium, past the art and music rooms, past the three-feet-by-two-feet canvases of Mother Teresa and the Reverend Martin Luther King Jr., toward the fifth-grade wing. Like the rest of the teachers, Mr. Morey waited outside of his room, C-4, at the far end of the hall. He wore an easy smile on his face. He was an optimist. He had to be. "Otherwise," he said, "I couldn't do my job."

Keith Morey liked to get to school early. Forty-one years old, he was in his tenth year of teaching, all at Brookside. He was one of just three male classroom teachers (the gym teacher was also male), and as such was a subject of curiosity among the students. Most had never had a male teacher. Rumor had it he ran his class differently from the other teachers. Many days, he arrived around eight A.M. In the quiet of his classroom, he'd grade the previous day's papers and do lesson prep. Often, he'd bring along Sean, the older of his two sons, now seven and a Brookside second grader. While the father worked, the son had the run of the classroom till the first students arrived. That meant raiding the Legos bin and constructing his vision of a postmodern world or tossing a ball he'd borrowed from the gym teacher.

On this day, Sean had more to do than his father did. Mr. Morey had spent parts of the previous week setting up his room, papering closet doors with vocabulary words, replenishing storage shelves with crayons and construction paper, and arranging a classroom library on the window shelf beside his desk. His last remaining task was to place name tags on each of the twenty-one desks, which he'd grouped in clusters of four and five, and spaced around the room. He thought back to his days after graduating from the State University of New York at New Paltz, when he had stayed on as the team's assistant basketball coach. Studying his class list, he felt as if he'd inherited a collection of players about whom he knew next to nothing. He hadn't queried their previous teachers about them. "I didn't want to start the year with preconceived notions," he said. A few names he recognized; he had taught their older siblings. The only other thing about them he knew was which kids to keep separated.

At nine A.M., Mr. Morey took up position outside his classroom door. He was dressed casually, in a navy polo shirt, tan slacks and slip-on shoes. As his students filed past, he handed each a sheet to fill out, titled "All About Me." Most reached for it without looking. They trained their eyes, instead, on Mr. Morey. Looking up at him was like staring straight up at the Empire State Building. Their teacher, tall and rangy, with the black, wavy hair of the Irish, effused a cool confidence. A minute passed before the children noticed the succession of 1980s hard-rock hits by Guns N' Roses and Queen that pulsed through the classroom. Mr. Morey was telling them a little about who he was. He was attempting to put them at ease.

Marbella walked into the room past Mr. Morey, uncertain what to read in his polite, "Good morning." She circled the desks like a wedding guest searching for her table. Mr. Morey had done his homework. He had separated the two rambunctious boys and the three chatty girls. Marbella found her seat at one of the clusters in the rear of the room, grouped with Josh, who was quiet and very bright; Sergio, who was quiet and exceedingly well behaved; and Monica, who was quiet and industrious, but sometimes derailed by her offbeat sense of humor. (Monica's mother, who spoke little

English, accompanied her daughter to class; at the door she searched for a way to communicate to Mr. Morey her desire that he keep her daughter in line. "You," she said to him—she shook a fist, indicating her child—"with Monica.") Marbella knew her three seatmates—they'd all attended Brookside for a year or more—but only casually. She eyed Hydea, already gabbing with Carlos, seated opposite her, and wondered if her group would get along as well.

The two had no idea that the machinery of the school was preparing to coalesce around them, that its key educators believed they and a handful of others on the cusp of reading proficiency could well determine during the March CMT whether Brookside would pass or continue to fail.

It wasn't all that long ago that the idea of Brookside failing was inconceivable. When the current building opened in 1952, it was known, said Mrs. Magrath, as "the country club on the hill." (The original building, a one-room schoolhouse, dated at least as far back as 1847.) In the 1980s Mrs. Magrath, who lived in another section of Norwalk, listed her Brookside-area babysitter as her children's caregiver so she could send them to school there. Then, as now, the surrounding neighborhood consisted of modest split-levels and single or two-family houses. The lots were small, but well kept. Diversity meant white-collar and blue-collar whites. An influx of poor and working-class Hispanics and blacks had settled along the northeast border of the neighborhood, but few of their children attended Brookside. Though the city had desegregated its schools in 1963, Brookside had remained at the time predominantly white, with a correspondingly white staff. "It was a high-achieving school, one of the best in [Norwalk]," Mrs. Magrath said. "You had a very active PTO, you had fund-raisers. You had a lot of parent involvement."

The classrooms were spacious. Its library stocked more than five thousand titles. The principal had been in place for years. That might have been the golden era of achievement at Brookside, and perhaps in Norwalk as well. Till then, as now, Norwalk's history regarding public education had not been an especially proud one.

At the time of its settlement, Connecticut had been at the forefront of the colonies regarding education. In 1650, its founder and first governor, Roger Ludlow, introduced the Ludlow Codes, a series of laws and practices that informed the framework of Connecticut's government. Ludlow considered education of such importance, he decreed that parents "endeavor to teach by themselves or others, their children and apprentices so much learning, as may enable them perfectly to read the English tongue, and knowledge of the capital laws, upon penalty of twenty shillings for each neglected therein." The code furthermore directed all towns of fifty or more households to hire a schoolteacher, and communities of one hundred families or more to establish a grammar school.

Ludlow had a particular interest in Norwalk. In 1640, he had purchased much of the land on which the town was later built. In 1652, a year after Norwalk was incorporated, the community hired Thomas Hanford, a non-ordained clergyman/New Haven schoolteacher, as its first schoolmaster. The following year, the town built him a wood-frame combination home/school/church meetinghouse that measured sixteen feet by thirty-one feet. By 1656, Hanford had so impressed the city fathers that they offered him the bountiful annual salary of £60, payable in wheat, barley, peas, pork, and beef. By the time Norwalk was ready to hire a new schoolmaster, though, in 1678, its generosity regarding public education had begun to change. That May, the town council voted to "hier a scole master to teach all the childring in the towne to lerne to rede and write," with instructions to "hier him upon as reasonable terms as they can."

The town did build the new teacher a freestanding schoolhouse, which opened in 1679. It consisted of a single room, twenty feet by eighteen feet, and was outfitted with a fireplace and backless wood benches. School ran Monday through Friday, plus half a day Saturday. The curriculum included Bible study, Latin grammar, and the dictionary, with writing considered the most important subject. Education in Norwalk was public then, but not free. Parents paid half the teacher's salary, plus a cord of wood for every two children they sent to school.

Things went downhill after that. By the early nineteenth century, Connecticut law required schools to teach reading, writing, and arithmetic as well as moral and religious instruction. To facilitate this, the state provided municipalities with a stipend to cover part of the cost. In most towns, it was understood that local taxes and fees would make up the balance. Norwalk, however, had other ideas. The townspeople, loathe to reach into their own pockets, decided that as much as possible, the annual state appropriation would have to suffice. One result was an absence of money for upkeep of its school buildings, which fell into disrepair over time. Another was the town's protracted, thirty-eight-year debate before finally allocating $38,500 to build its first high school, in

1909. For decades, the schools didn't even provide textbooks. Parents had to purchase their own at local bookstores. Families too poor to afford them generally kept their children home. The community was untroubled by this till late in the nineteenth century, when townspeople learned state education funds would henceforth be tied to school attendance. Norwalk speedily voted to provide free textbooks to all—with the proviso that new ones would not be purchased for another ten years.

This flintiness extended to the schoolteachers. For most of the nineteenth century, the surest way to land a Norwalk teaching job was to undercut the lowest bid on the table. By 1928, the town's reputation for niggardly pay was such that one teacher made front-page news when she quit her job for one an hour's train ride away in New York City that promised a thousand dollars more. Nineteen years later, in 1947, the *New York Times* reported that the average single female Norwalk teacher earned $2,218, which was $99 a year less than her expected annual living expenses.

Things began to change after World War II, when millions of returning servicemen took advantage of the G.I. Bill to attend college. For the first time, higher education became accessible to a broad swath of Americans who previously had considered it out of reach. This new class of college graduates wanted the same, and better, for their own children, the generation that would become known as the baby boomers. They pushed local school boards across the nation to improve public education—to invest in new school buildings, cutting-edge teaching materials, and better-educated teachers.

In Norwalk, this meant a spate of building. Brookside's current building opened in 1952. Brien McMahon High School, a third of a mile down the street, opened in 1960. Roton Middle School, two-thirds of a mile still farther along the same street, was christened in 1966, creating a kind of education row. This worked out well for the Brookside kids, who would spend all their public school years along one small stretch of road.

What Norwalk didn't push was its 1963 desegregation plan. Much of the town's black and Hispanic population was concentrated in the South Norwalk district, a warren of subdivided houses, public housing, and rundown, ramshackle apartments that abutted Norwalk's downtown. The town's initial hope was to retain as much as possible the integrity of its neighborhood school system, busing only those minority children living in South Norwalk to achieve racial parity. "City officials worried that if they bused white children, there'd be white flight," said Ralph Sloan, Norwalk's schools superintendent from 1983 to 1998. Implementation was painfully slow. As late as 1979, most of the city's then-sixteen elementary schools, including Brookside, remained disproportionately white, whereas the South Norwalk, downtown-area schools were predominantly Hispanic and black. Columbus Elementary School, located in the heart of South Norwalk, had a minority population of 87 percent. The school board, under pressure, closed two of its minority-laden elementary schools and in 1980 converted Columbus to a magnet school.

That meant hundreds of elementary school students had to be bused to other schools, including Brookside. During this period, the neighborhood's population began to change, as well. The number of subdivided residences increased. Some whites did flee. Others transferred their children to religious or private schools. By the start of the 2010–11 school year, Mrs. Magrath's "country club on the hill" was 21 percent white and 76 percent Hispanic and black. It still lacked racial parity.

M r. Morey followed the last arriving student into the room and shut the door. After the pledge of allegiance, the daily moment of silence and morning announcements, he strode to the front of the classroom and surveyed his new students. He was under no illusions. He had completed both his internship and student teaching assignments in Redding, Connecticut, a suburban community of about nine thousand that in 2010 was 95 percent white, with an average household income of $207,000 (60 percent of those households earned $125,000 or more) and where the idea of a failing school wasn't even a thought. Three months later he landed his first full-time job, at Brookside, just eighteen miles south. It was hard to think that those few miles could spell such a difference. But now, having taught there nine years, he knew with certainty the hand he'd been dealt. The lack of money changed things, sure. But it was the number of single-parent families, the transiency, the parents unversed in English who were unable to help their children with homework, the general absence of books or other reading materials in their homes, the unworldliness of students who had never been to a museum or zoo—even their limited dreams of community college and a trade—that separated the two towns. At that start of the school year, it was hard not to feel his students were already behind. Some, including Marbella and Hydea, were startled by the way Mr. Morey looked at them and felt a shiver of uncertainty. Why was their teacher staring? Was he upset with them already? Mr. Morey held his gaze another beat. It was an effective technique for establishing control. But that wasn't his primary goal. Watching the children, he wondered as he does on the first day of each school year, *Do they want to be here?*

Mr. Morey was pretty sure he knew the answer from his own family background. In many ways, his upbringing wasn't all that different from that of his students. He grew up in Staten Island, one of New York City's working-class, outer boroughs, where he was raised in lower-middle-class circumstances by a father employed as a sanitation worker and a mother who worked as a dental assistant at a state mental-health institution. His parents, high school graduates, divorced when he was three. He lived with his mother till age twelve, then moved in with his dad. "I wasn't really the best kid," Mr. Morey explained. "I wasn't listening very much. It was just getting to be too much for my mom."

When he was thirteen, he moved upstate with his dad to Brewster, New York, a village of about twenty-two hundred where in 2010 fewer than half the residents over age twenty-five had attended college. Like many of his Brookside students, Mr. Morey moved from school to school, attending seven by the time he graduated from high school. His grades weren't great. "I was an average student, maybe a little above average. I didn't push myself," he recalled. In high school his grades would slide and his father would threaten to pull him from the baseball team, at which point, he said, "my grades would miraculously get better." His toughest challenge, with all the shifting around, was winning acceptance, making friends. When his dad divorced a second time, before his senior year in high school, precipitating a move to yet another school, he lost almost all interest in school. "Moving my senior year really changed a lot of things for me," Mr. Morey recalled. "It took my focus off of college. I was just mad. I can't remember one teacher from my senior year. I've just blanked it out." After graduation, he enlisted in the air force. It took him years, he said, to find his bearings, to figure out what he wanted to do with his life. Now, standing in front of his students, he felt an ability to relate to them in ways his colleagues perhaps couldn't.

Like the other fifth-grade teachers, Mr. Morey hadn't had any say over the makeup of his class. That had been largely the task of the fourth-grade teachers, who'd met near the end of the previous school term to divvy up their students among the fifth-grade faculty, assigning to each, as nearly as possible, an equal number of top students and slower ones; disruptive children and model ones; boys and girls; and blacks, Hispanics, and whites. In June they had submitted their proposed class lists to Mr. Hay, who had proceeded as he did every year, some teachers groused, to unravel what they'd done. Mr. Hay was a notorious soft touch, and when a parent or grandparent or one of the volunteers from the student mentoring program asked that a child be placed with a particular teacher, he would almost always oblige. Among the three fifth-grade teachers, Mr. Morey and Mrs. Keefe received the bulk of these requests—Mr. Morey, because he is male; Mrs. Keefe, because of her reputation for throwing classroom parties. Throughout the summer Mr. Hay maneuvered students like numbers on a Sudoku grid, seeking to rebalance the three classes.

In this way, Mr. Morey picked up Fernando, a short, slender, often disruptive ten-year-old who had been a handful ever since matriculating at Brookside as a kindergartner. He also inherited the six students the inexperienced fourth-grade teacher had been unable to control. Mr. Morey took this as a compliment, a sign of Mr. Hay's trust. It was his job, he believed, to motivate children like these to learn. Whether he'd succeed was another question. Sometimes he wasn't even certain of his own son's interest in school: Sean, who was raised in a family that celebrated education. Mr. Morey's eyes swept the room. The students were silent, wary. Even the bolder boys were uncertain how to behave.

"You have the opportunity to show me who you are," Mr. Morey began. "If you cause trouble, you're showing me who you are." His no-nonsense style threw them. They were used to being nurtured. Perhaps Mr. Morey wasn't the good-guy teacher he was reputed to be. The students shifted in their seats. Five were African American, seven were white, nine Hispanic. There were ten boys, eleven girls. They mirrored the general Brookside population. A little more than half qualified for free or reduced-fee school lunches, of which about three-quarters were minority students. Five lived with a single parent or grandparent. None could be classified as wealthy. "Maybe a couple of parents in the entire school earn a hundred thousand," Mr. Hay said.

Mr. Morey laid down the ground rules. No one was to talk till they raised a hand and were acknowledged. In addition to their regular homework, students were required to read thirty minutes per night, ten minutes longer than they had in fourth grade. It was the students' job to organize, by genre, the two-hundred-book classroom library. Those stuck on a problem were encouraged to seek his help, but children who sought assistance before even trying would receive none at all. "You're fifth graders now. Next year you'll be in middle school. I'm not going to baby you," Mr. Morey said.

At that point, he opened the floor to questions. There were two.

"Do we need to sign a paper to go to the bathroom?" asked Carlos. He kept his hand raised, indicating he had a follow-up: "When we have snack time, do we also get to go the bathroom?"

Mr. Morey did not change expression. A good part of his evolution as a teacher had involved knowing when to draw the line with a student and when to let things slide. Above all, he had learned never to register shock or surprise. To do so would reveal weakness, tantamount to ceding control.

Carlos. So now he knew the identity of one of his potential irritants. He reminded himself: These are ten-year-olds. Yes, there would be bathroom breaks, he said, addressing the class rather than the cheeky boy. Without breaking stride, he moved on to the next piece of business. Mrs. Schaefer had requested that each fifth-grade teacher assign an in-class writing exercise to establish a baseline assessment of each student's ability. Mr. Morey reviewed the concept of a narrative story—a form introduced to Brookside students in second grade—and then asked that they compose one of their own. "It can be about anything," he said. "It can be about a soccer game, or something your pet did, or about going to the mall." A competent fifth grader, he knew, should be able to complete this type of assignment in fifteen minutes. He gave them forty-five.

Mr. Morey returned to his desk in the left front corner of the room. He had organized it as a man would: functional, as opposed to neat. Scattered on it, and extending over a double stack of file cabinets pressed flush to its side, were administrative memos, curriculum guidebooks, family photos, paperback children's novels, student handouts, scrawled notes to himself—the flotsam of his profession. At the center of the desk in the one spot free of clutter sat a computer. Every Brookside teacher had one, provided by the school. Not all were expert in its use. Mr. Morey, who'd served in the air force as an electronics technician, was perhaps the most tech-savvy person on staff. More or less by default, he'd become the school's unofficial IT consultant, a kind of one-man Geek Squad whom other teachers sought out (sometimes during school hours, interrupting whatever lesson he happened to be teaching) when flummoxed by a new software program or when their computer crashed. From time to time he had toyed with starting a side business training teachers how to access and implement the latest in educational software. Maybe one day he'd finally get around to doing it. For now, he sat and faced his monitor, pretending to check his e-mail and surf the Web. Mr. Morey smiled to himself, thinking about that TV show *Are You Smarter Than a Fifth Grader?* He could at least outwit one. For the next half-hour, he sneaked peaks at his new students to judge both their work ethic and their stamina for writing.

His class reminded him of an out-of-shape hoops team that hadn't practiced in months. Yesica, an English as a second language (ESL) student so painfully shy that she spoke in a whisper, had trouble getting started. Aajah, a tall, effervescent free spirit who'd qualified for the academically talented class that met once a week, paused after writing eight lines to shake out her exhausted right hand. Dennis, a slender, spiky-haired boy who had moved to Norwalk the previous year, devoted three minutes to writing four brief sentences about his rec league soccer team before setting down his pencil. Hydea was one of the few students who filled a full page.

Hydea couldn't believe her luck. Of all the subjects Mr. Morey could have chosen, story writing was the single one in which she felt confident. Not in the kind of writing where the teacher asked you to explain the meaning of someone else's story, like the ones printed in her language arts handouts. Those gave her trouble. Sometimes she could sort of *say* what they were about, but she stumbled trying to translate her thoughts to paper. What she was good at was writing her own make-believe stories. In fact, she had just told Aajah about this magical, Alice in Wonderland–like world she'd created, called Rabia. In Rabia, everybody had rabies, though nobody got sick from it. Hydea couldn't say exactly where it was located. She just liked how the word sounded.

Aajah, Hydea's best friend since kindergarten, had been mesmerized. Immediately, she had wanted to go. "I told her that to get to Rabia, you have to go to this secret place," Hydea said. "There's this big hole by the secret place, and then you crawl down a ladder, and then there's a swamp and you have to cross the swamp and it leads to this underground street. You go down the street and then there's these underground woods. You gotta cross the woods and there's this big, weird-looking place that you go into, and that's a pet shop. You go through the door and everything in the room is white, and there's these voices you hear that say, 'Hello!' And then you hear huge footsteps and a giant comes out, and you think he's all scary and mean, but he's really nice. His name is Chubby."

Hydea didn't write about Rabia for Mr. Morey, though. She didn't really know Mr. Morey, and was afraid he'd find it silly. Instead, she composed a variation of the same piece she'd been sharing with teachers since first grade: Her most recent two-week summer trip to Atlanta to see her dad, a housepainter. She filled the page with the excursions they took: to see her cousins, to a playground in a nearby park, to hike Georgia's Stone Mountain.

Marbella chose a travel theme for her story, too. She squirmed in her seat, stuck for what to write till she remembered her family's summer visit to Block Island, a vacation destination off the Rhode Island coast. There was a lot to tell about: the house where they stayed, the different white-sand beaches, and a great ice cream parlor they stopped at called The Ice Cream Place. Marbella set pencil to paper. Unlike Hydea, she took no special pleasure in doing so. She didn't like writing better than any other subject, except maybe social studies, and only then around Thanksgiving, when they got to dress up like the pilgrims and learn about the Native Americans who helped them survive. She just wanted to get the exercise over with.

After about twenty minutes, Marbella exhaled and pushed her paper aside. She didn't bother rereading her work. Neither did Hydea. Only one member of the class did. Mr. Morey collected the papers and riffled through them without comment. Experience had taught him not to expect much. Without exception, he noted, each of their stories had been organized into a single, Faulknerian-length paragraph, unrelieved by commas, periods, indentation, or capitalization. Grammar and tenses had been mangled. They'd paid scant attention to spelling. Would became *whould*. Problem became *promble*. Though the students had studied cursive writing since second grade, none had used it. Hydea couldn't remember the last time she'd even practiced it. One boy, across the hall in Mrs. Bohrer's class, couldn't read the homework assignment the teacher had written in script that afternoon on the whiteboard. Mr. Morey marveled, as he did every year, how children could forget so much over the ten short weeks of summer vacation, even the brighter ones. According to Mrs. Schaefer, those who skipped summer reading often saw their reading levels slip. ESL learners who went the summer without reading, she said, could slip by as much as half a grade level. Of course, for some, forgetfulness wasn't the problem. It was clear to Mr. Morey that a number of his students had simply arrived in his classroom unschooled in the basics.

It didn't take long for the students to find their fit in Mr. Morey's class. Josh and Kyle, a tall, crew-cut blond who was popular because he was both bright and a good athlete, were the two who most often volunteered answers and were right. Carlos, born in the United States and raised by his Colombian mother, was the most likely to raise his hand and be silly or wrong. Josh's best friend, Chris, who drew comics built around the superhero characters he created, often had his head in the clouds. Sara, who planned to be a fashion designer, struggled with math but was the class's best writer. Jacky, the most dedicated student, lacked the confidence to raise her hand in class, but when called on generally knew the answer; her Guatemalan parents, who met while working at a local ShopRite, had high hopes Jacky would someday be a lawyer. Yesica and Hydea never raised their hands, Yesica out of shyness, Hydea for fear she'd embarrass herself by answering incorrectly. Marbella raised her hand to please Mr. Morey, but prayed he wouldn't call on her. Fernando, who was immature and disruptive, was quickly separated from his pod and forced to sit alone at the front of the room. So was Dennis, who balked at doing classwork, and yet who dreamed of being an architect, even convincing his parents to hire him a math tutor because he had read it was a necessary skill for designing buildings. The majority just kept their heads down, hoping Mr. Morey wouldn't call on them.

Mr. Morey had a routine, too. He liked to teach language arts and math early in the day, while his students still had energy and focus. At lunchtime, he recharged his own batteries. While the other fifth-grade teachers dined in the faculty room, he drove to his home less than a mile away, to his younger son and waiting wife. Half an hour was all he had. Upon his return, he allotted the students fifteen minutes for independent reading from books they selected from the classroom library, while he prepared their next lesson. Generally, he taught a second round of language arts or math, and a non-core subject, such as social studies or science. Around three P.M., if he had time, he gathered the students on the rug in the front of the room and read them a chapter from *Cirque du Freak*, a popular book series about a boy's descent into the bloody world of vampires. Among both boys and girls, horror was the preferred genre. (Chris chose a HorrorLand book for his independent reading; Sara, *The Big Book of Horror*; Sergio, *Scary Creatures: Hippos*.) But Mr. Morey seldom had the opportunity to read aloud.

One of Mr. Morey's first and most important realizations was how little actual teaching time he had. School began at 9:05 A.M., but class didn't effectively start till the conclusion of the Pledge of Allegiance and the morning announcements, at 9:25. On a typical day, the children might have gym from 9:52 to 10:22. Snack time was ten minutes, starting at 11 A.M. Recess ran from 12:45 to 1 P.M., followed by lunch. Chorus might go from 1:42 to 2:42. Other days, they might break for art, music, the computer room, or library time. At 3:15 in the afternoon, Mr. Morey sent the students to their lockers to gather their coats and book bags. Dismissal was at 3:25. That left three hours and twenty-five minutes for learning—minus the time lost when the children rummaged through their desks for their workbooks and homework, when they took bathroom breaks, and when they grew noisy and Mr. Morey had to call for order.

Most days, Mr. Morey didn't know where the time went. It wasn't just a matter of covering the material set out in the school's curriculum guide. The biggest part of his job, he had come to realize, was teaching his students to think independently. After one lackluster writing exercise, he went home, flipped on the TV to a Yankees game and let his mind wander as he often did, wondering how to get through to them. In the background, he heard Sean and his four-year-old brother, Sebastian, playing, and he tried to time travel back to when he was an elementary school kid. Sometimes, he said, an idea would pop into his head and a kind of alchemy would take place. The heart of the solution was always the same. "If you want something to stick, you've got to teach it in terms of their everyday lives," he said. He recalled an idea the district's language arts chief had mentioned several years before. The next morning, as soon as school announcements ended, Mr. Morey called the class to the rug in front of the room and outlined what looked like a Sherlock Holmes–style pipe on the whiteboard and placed five Xs on and around it. He turned to the class. "This is the street where I grew up, the cul-de-sac where all my buddies and I lived," he said. "All my greatest memories from that time are here, and I've marked them with these exes." He pointed to one of the marks near the bottom of the pipe. "This was my house. We had a pretty big backyard that ran right along a stone wall and some woods. One day I took a hatchet and chopped a BMX trail for my bike. It was this great up-and-down trail I rode all the time." Mr. Morey pointed to a second mark, this one to the side of the pipe. "This was my friend John's house, down the street from me. He had this big lawn on the side of his house, and at night it was lit up by a streetlight and a floodlight. That's where we played night football in the fall." He attached a memory to each of the *X*s. The students were rapt. It was like listening to campfire stories, and learning about their teacher at the same time.

"Boys and girls," Mr. Morey said, "yesterday many of you had trouble figuring out what to write. But you have stories all around you, just like me. Go back to your seats and take out your writing notebooks and turn to an empty page. Draw a picture of your neighborhood, or your home, or even Brookside, where a lot of you have been coming for years. Wherever you pick, you'll find places to put exes, places where your best memories are. Any questions?"

Kyle raised his hand. Eleven o'clock was approaching. "When is snack time?" he asked.

Mr. Morey let the remark pass. He could tell from scanning the room: Most of the students got it. They set to work filling their notebooks with line drawings and *X*s, jotting keywords, clearly engaged. Mr. Morey returned to his desk and watched them, taking it all in. *This is a teaching moment*, he thought. *Enjoy it.* He plopped down in his chair, laced his fingers behind his head, allowed himself to relax. He glanced at the wall clock. Oh, man. The lesson had taken half an hour, and he'd allotted the students forty minutes more of writing time. His language arts period would run way long. Something would have to give. Too often, some lesson had to give. Today it would have to be science. Unlike some teachers, Mr. Morey enjoyed teaching the subject. He admired its orderliness, its ability to explain the mechanics of space, of sound, of the seasons, of life. But science wasn't a core subject at Brookside, as were reading, writing, and math. He'd planned to teach two science lessons that week. He'd probably get to just one. And it would only get worse come January, when CMT prep began and science was even further marginalized. He pushed the thought aside. He had a more immediate concern. In forty minutes the students would lay down their pencils, and he'd have to conjure a way to inspire them anew.

Chapter 2

Late September 2010

Marbella and Hydea didn't devote much thought to their classroom, where they spent such a large chunk of their day. It was pretty much like every other room they'd been assigned to since coming to Brookside. Maybe the desks were arranged differently and the teacher hung pictures of the solar system on the walls, rather than posters bearing inspirational messages. The only real difference in Mr. Morey's room was the SMART Board that dominated the front wall—an Internet-connected whiteboard that enabled Mr. Morey to teach lessons via the Web and write notes in digital ink. His was the only fifth-grade room to have one. Otherwise, it was stocked with items common to every upper-grades classroom: Five HP desktop computers spaced along the side and back walls, on which students played educational games during snack time and before class. Maps of the world. Shoe boxes filled with Legos. A well-stocked classroom library. A parti-colored area rug at the front of the room where students gathered for lessons or to listen to Mr. Morey read stories. Storage cubbies, for whatever didn't fit in their desks. A water fountain and sink.

The girls didn't realize how different things had been in August 2003, when their older siblings had attended the school and Mr. Hay first arrived. Mr. Hay's initial impression was that Brookside was less school building than construction site. He drove there shortly before his final interview with then–school superintendent Salvatore Corda, after he had pretty much been assured the principal's position. "I pulled up in front of the school," he recalled. "It was a few weeks before school was scheduled to start, and there was this huge, twenty-by-forty-foot hole in the front of the building. There's dirt mounds everywhere, and there's Sheetrock scattered around. I said, hmmm, this is my new building? I went around to the back, and lo and behold, the same thing. It looked like a demolition job."

Brookside was in the midst of an eighteen-month renovation that was long overdue. The forty-nine-year-old building was dark, dingy looking, leaked rainwater, had an air-quality problem (many students and faculty suffered persistent sinus infections), and was infested with ants. ("Mrs. Freeman's room was across from mine," Mrs. Magrath said. "I remember putting a sign on a chair in the hallway: Ants Go East. And she put a sign on a chair: Ants Go West.") The gym and cafeteria were unusable; students lunched in their classrooms. That fall, the fourth and fifth graders were relocated to temporary classrooms in the rear parking lot. The only way for teachers to communicate with the main office was by foot. The library was shuttered. Almost all its ten thousand books had been shipped to a Bridgeport, Connecticut, warehouse for storage. The librarian, Mrs. Madden, kept perhaps one hundred titles, which she supplemented with books from the children's collection in the Norwalk Public Library. "I borrowed books on a weekly basis on my own library card," she recalled. "I rolled a library cart from class to class and read the books to the children, half an hour a week per class. They didn't have books to borrow." And those were only the most visible of the school's problems.

At his final interview with Mr. Corda, said Mr. Hay, "The superintendent sat me down and he proceeded to talk. He didn't ask questions. He proceeded to describe what he thought Brookside was at that point. He stated to me, number one, that the school, testing-wise, was one of the worst in the city, if not at the bottom. That the previous administrator had left and there was a great deal of turmoil accompanying her departure. A certain percentage of the staff supported her and a larger percentage didn't. He said there was in-house fighting, that there were a lot of battles going on in the building at the faculty level. Also, he said the parents were up in arms about the whole situation and were trying to control things."

Corda didn't stop there. He informed Mr. Hay that the school district had adopted a complete new curriculum for the coming term, supplanting one that had been in place for approximately fifteen years. Mr. Hay inquired which subject would be updated first. Typically, a school rolls out one redesigned course per year. It takes at least that long for a staff to master the new material and how to teach it. Installing an across-the-board curriculum is generally a five-to-seven-year process. To Mr. Hay's surprise, Mr. Corda replied they were replacing all the courses at once—language arts, math, social studies, and science. The superintendent paused a beat. "Are you interested in the position?" he asked.

It struck Mr. Hay that the superintendent could have been describing the chaos of any one of ten thousand U.S. public schools. Around the time of his interview with Dr. Corda, the San Jose (California) United School District laid off all twenty-two of its librarians. Parents at the city's Hacienda Elementary School made headlines when they contributed $52,000 to keep Dayle Moore, their longtime school librarian, on the job. Moore, a thirty-four-year staff veteran, recently had been named the district's Teacher of the Year. In 2008, the *Wall Street Journal* would report that the high school graduation rate in America's top fifty cities had dropped to 52 percent, the lowest-ranked being Detroit, at 25 percent. In February 2010, the Central Falls, Rhode Island, school board would vote to fire all eighty-seven or so faculty and staff members at chronically underperforming Central Falls High. Later that year, the state of Connecticut would celebrate its best standardized test results since the inception of NCLB, with the announcement that it had reduced to "just" 28 percent the number of its schools that were out of academic compliance. "Clearly, we see progress in these results," then–state education commissioner Mark McQuillan would say.

The Norwalk superintendent waited for an answer. Mr. Hay didn't hesitate. He had applied to nineteen Connecticut school districts and had received just two other offers, neither of which had excited him. "Yeah, it sounds good," he said. Mr. Hay liked challenges, and this one bore little risk. "I recognized that I couldn't do much worse than what they had at that point," he told a friend.

W hen Mr. Hay thought about how his life had turned out, he had to smile. Unlike most Brookside faculty members and administrators, he didn't grow up dreaming of being an educator. Coming out of high school, he wasn't sure what he wanted to be. He was a good baseball pitcher, but not talented enough to play professionally. Home was Ashby, Massachusetts, then a rural village of eighteen hundred that hugged the New Hampshire border in the central part of the state. His father helped run Fitchburg Plumbing Supply, the family's wholesale plumbing supply business. His mother worked there, too. Mr. Hay could have joined them, but he wanted something else. His options seemed limited. He was a B student and not a very dedicated one at that, graduating seventeenth in a class of twenty-six. He was tall and skinny and so shy he dropped his head and blushed crimson whenever called on in class. His timidity led him to attend Fitchburg State College (now Fitchburg State University), less than ten miles from his home.

At the time, Fitchburg State was known primarily for its teaching and nursing programs. Teaching didn't seem to fit his character. For lack of other alternatives, Mr. Hay chose it anyway. A lover of history, he figured he'd teach the subject at the high school or middle school level. A family friend who taught at the college recommended that he major in elementary education instead. Because elementary schools were always looking for male teachers, he'd be more likely to find a job, the friend said.

He began his career in 1969 at George Street Elementary

School (now shuttered), a predominantly white, relatively affluent public school in nearby Leominster, Massachusetts. Primarily, he taught fifth- and sixth-grade math. He was a curiosity from the start, not only to the students but to the faculty, a number of whom were near retirement. It was more than his being the sole male teacher. It was his look, his image. "I was a twenty-two-year-old kid with long hair and a fast car—a big, bright red Plymouth Roadrunner, a muscle car," he said. "I wore bell-bottom jeans and a fur coat, was six feet and maybe a hundred forty-five pounds."

Mr. Hay had thirty-five students in his first class, and quickly realized he had little idea how to teach them. A school of education was like law school, he decided. Both were excellent at imparting theory, but less so at arming students with practical skills. "Colleges don't teach you about curriculum," he said. "You were basically one step in front of the kids, because you'd never seen any of these textbooks before in your life. So you're learning just ahead of them and you're trying to make everything right. It's hard, because you're teaching all day. There weren't a lot of breaks in those days. You didn't have a lot of prep time." The veteran teachers helped some, but mostly he felt his way along.

From the start, Mr. Hay experimented. Bashful among adults, he came alive around his students. The young teacher discovered a creativity he hadn't known he'd had. He taught math through card games, rolled dice to teach probability. He took his class to a local rock quarry to learn about minerals. Every few months he reconfigured his classroom seating, for both the students and himself. For a while he plunked his desk in the center of the room, smack in the middle of the children. Often, he lunched with them in the cafeteria. During recess he refereed their basketball games. One day a parent spotted him running on the playground. "Wow, that's a big kid for sixth grade," she told her son.

Mr. Hay taught a total of eighteen years at three Leominster elementary schools. Like any teacher, he had his weaknesses. Though an avid reader, he lacked confidence teaching language arts. And early on, despite his popularity, he had trouble controlling students. "I was a yeller," he said. He had had his own Fernandos and Carloses. Decades later, the missteps he made remained fresh in his mind. "[Your students are] making noise, you make more noise just to quiet them down," he recalled, sitting in his Brookside office. "You punish them, and then they do it again and you punish them more and it snowballs until pretty soon they owe you, like, a thousand days after school and you go, I didn't win. It took me over a year and a half before I even started to get it. I got quieter, learned to pick my battles. It took me about seven years to really learn the craft."

Mr. Hay did have one special classroom skill from the start: taking second-tier math students and driving them to outperform the top ones. "There are certain groups that, as a teacher, you're drawn to," he said. "If you can get any spark out of them, it's great. I would challenge them and say, 'Listen, that [top] group thinks they're better than you, but you can beat them.'"

Mr. Hay was demanding. Each morning began with a multiplication quiz—a page of eighty-one problems and with a goal of solving them in one hundred seconds. He'd point to a student. "Six times nine," he'd say, and snap his fingers once, twice. "What's the answer?" It became a daily competition. Because the children liked Mr. Hay, and because he turned multiplication into a game, they strove to please him. Afterward came the day's new lesson.

Mr. Hay employed a technique uncommon in Leominster schools at the time. He individualized their instruction, a strategy he never attempted with any other subject, including language arts. "We'd be studying fractions," he said, "and there'd be one kid on page fifty-two [in the text] and another on page forty-six. The kids were all over the place. Maybe three would come up to me and I'd give them a five-minute mini-lesson and they'd go back and do the work. Everyone went at their own pace. The ones who wanted to fly went zoom. There was no waiting. It motivated the kids to achieve their highest level." Many did, passing students in the top tier.

The end of each math period, Mr. Hay recalled, left him spent, exhausted. "It was non-stop working. I couldn't have maintained that rate through the entire day," he said. But the pride and pleasure he took from those class sessions transported him, even in the years he struggled with class management. He left school each afternoon feeling an athlete's high. He was a man in love with his job.

Mr. Hay might have remained an elementary school teacher throughout his career, had not marriage (to his high school sweetheart) and three children ensued. He applied for his first administrative job, he said, because he needed money to support his growing family. His teacher's salary had never amounted to much: $6,300 his first year, $33,000 in his final one (he earned an additional $1,000 for serving as vice president of the local teachers union and $2,000 more from a state educational grant). He'd always had to work a second and sometimes a third supplemental job. When the school day ended, he hustled to the Goody-Goody Café in Fitchburg, a shot-and-a-beer joint, his family's other business, where he served as manager. Summers found him at the plumbing supply company working maintenance when not at the bar.

In 1987 Mr. Hay took a risk, agreeing to a $3,000 pay cut to become assistant principal at Priest Street, a troubled Leominster elementary school on the poorer, west side of town. (It too has since closed.) He was fortunate to be hired; at the time he lacked certification as a public school administrator. It took him eight more years, two more vice principalships, and another cut in pay to land his first principal's position, at Baldwinville Elementary School, in Baldwinville, Massachusetts (population two thousand), twenty-two miles west of Leominster. He worked there two years before returning to Leominster to run Fall Brook Elementary School. He stayed at that school six years before leaving for Brookside.

Baldwinville had just twelve teachers and roughly 320 students. Fall Brook, the largest elementary school in its district, had thirty-six teachers and a student population that topped 1,000. The three other Massachusetts schools where he served as an administrator fell somewhere in between. Mr. Hay saw a commonality to them. All were schools with poor reputations. Their staffs were fractious and unhappy, their students underperformed, and there seemed no improvement in sight. "The culture in every building was terrible," he recalled. That's why the jobs had opened up. At Baldwinville, he said, "I remember very clearly going into the [former principal's desk] drawer and there was a stack of papers about a foot and a half high, and it was all memos to the staff, and they were all do-not memos. Do not do that, do not do this. And I said to myself, they must get a memo or two a day with do-nots. Sometimes the do-nots went to everybody, even when it was only meant for one person." At Fall Brook, "there were thirty-six classrooms and thirty-six closed doors." Priest Street, he said, was saddled with a dyspeptic principal whose sour attitude permeated the school. "He once won ten thousand dollars in a contest," Mr. Hay said, "and his only response was, 'Why me?' Because he thought, 'Everybody's going to bother me for money now.'"

By the time he applied for the Brookside position, Mr. Hay had come to a simple conclusion about the nature of a dysfunctional school: Change cannot occur as long as the staff is preoccupied with internal strife, and change takes time. In his experience, it took a minimum of two years to begin to turn a building around. Job one at a troubled school, as he saw it, was to coax teachers to cooperate as a team. This had not been easy. In every building in which he had worked, the reservoir of distrust and discontent had run deep. The shy man had been forced to lead. At Baldwinville, he built a school library (later named for him). At Fall Brook he opened his office door, and told teachers he wanted their doors open, too. In ways big and small, Mr. Hay placed himself front and center. He picked up a mop and helped the custodians clean the hallways and cafeteria. He announced a schoolwide book-reading challenge: Exceed the combined total he set for the school, and he'd spend an entire spring day seated on the roof, reading— which he subsequently did. He cadged money to buy SMART Boards and desktop computers for the classrooms. He initiated a Reading Recovery program, an intensive, innovative strategy for identifying slow first-grade readers and tutoring them, one-on-one, till they reached grade level. He was game for anything that would improve the school's atmosphere and standing. Thinking back to his second year of teaching, he recalled, "A little girl said, 'Mr. Hay, why don't you smile?' I could have easily blown it off, but I thought about what she said. She was right, saying I should smile when I walked down the hall. So I started to practice it in the mirror at home. I'd wake up and say to myself, you gotta smile today. It got so I wanted everybody in school to smile more. When you smile, there's something chemical that happens in your brain. When you smile, it's pretty hard to do something bad or think evil thoughts about people. You feel good about yourself."

Over time, his Massachusetts schools turned around. At Fall Brook, the first visible sign of change occurred when the school's lackadaisical head custodian left. Mr. Hay hired an energetic replacement, and almost overnight the school grew cleaner and brighter. Some of the more ineffectual teachers transferred or retired. At Mr. Hay's urging, those who remained began to work together. They began mentoring the new teachers, experimenting with strategies for improving classroom instruction, demanding more of their students. Mr. Hay, the man who related more readily to children, made clear that student welfare was his overriding concern. He initiated a successful, two-way bilingual program, where Spanish-speaking students populated English-speaking classes, and English-speaking students attended classes conducted in Spanish. Standardized test scores improved. In his final years at Fall Brook, "Education gurus started to drop by, to see what we were doing," Mr. Hay said. "I had a terrific gym teacher, a librarian who was asked to go to other schools and show what she was doing, and a literacy person who was asked to do the same. We had good people. They just had to come out of their doors."

Mr. Hay had felt well prepared when he arrived at Brookside. But the picture was worse than what Superintendent Corda had painted. The school's standardized test scores were not just among the lowest in the city. They were getting worse. Each year, several of its top students were opting out of the building and enrolling at other schools, further dragging down Brookside's composite test scores. The faculty was more than discontented; it was wracked by schism.

Mr. Hay's predecessor had been forced to negotiate a separation agreement with the board of education, ending her principalship a month before the end of the 2002–03 school term. The woman had served a little less than two years. A petition signed by most of the school's teachers had demanded her removal. During her tenure, CMT scores had plunged along with student behavior. Most teachers attributed it to her lax management style, which had polarized the staff. "She delegated everything," Mrs. Keefe, one of the principal's few supporters, recalled. Teachers complained that Planning and Placement Team meetings for learning-disabled students went unscheduled because the principal neglected to send parents the required paperwork. They also said they received little or no support when disciplinary problems arose. In one instance, a hard-to-control boy threw his chair against the wall and then grabbed Mrs. Magrath's left arm and twisted it behind her back, separating her shoulder—the second time he had attacked her that year. (In the first instance, the boy had shoved a desk into her, bruising her stomach.) Mrs. Magrath claimed that when she made her way to the principal's office and demanded that she phone the boy's parents and initiate transfer proceedings, the principal balked. "You call his mother," Mrs. Magrath recalled the principal saying, not wishing to make the call herself.

The principal's apparent disengagement extended to the classroom. According to a number of faculty members, she had no action plan to reverse the school's tumbling scores. Teachers said they felt little pressure to work hard or to ensure that their students achieved. "She would just tell us, 'Do whatever you want and don't bother me,' basically," Bonnie Lindsay, one of the special education teachers, said. Sometimes, teachers claimed, the principal arrived late to school; often, they added, she left the moment the clock struck four, the earliest her contract allowed, long before many of the staff. The principal, many believed, was shirking her duty. The faculty split over the issue. The eight or so who supported her were ostracized. That, perhaps, was the principal's most devastating impact on the school. The faculty stopped being a team. "One day," said a teacher who was among those shunned, "I threw a wheel of brie into the teachers' lounge and I wrote, 'For the two-legged rats that live in here.'"

Like the rest of the faculty, Mr. Morey didn't know what to expect of Mr. Hay when, the day before the 2003–04 school term began, the new principal introduced himself to the staff. At the time, Mr. Morey had been teaching two years and had served under one full-time and two interim principals. He was still trying to get comfortable in his job. During the faculty strife the previous year, he had kept his head down, concentrating on his class, and had tried not to get politically involved. "I didn't really know anybody," he recalled. "I would talk to Miss Montgomery, the ESL teacher, because she was right next door to me, and to Mrs. Freeman, one of the fifth-grade teachers, but it wasn't like an open community. It seemed like every teacher did their own thing. For me, there were a lot of questions in the air. Not just about Mr. Hay's teaching philosophy and what that was going to mean for me, but how long was he going to stay? Was he going to be here for a year or two like the others?"

Mr. Hay had sensed the staff's unease the moment he stood to speak. Before the meeting, he had scoured the Internet, reading local newspaper reports and minutes from recent school board hearings, trying to get a feel for what he was up against. Now, in the cramped space that prior to construction had served as the school library, he could feel the contention coming through.

Mr. Hay addressed the staff matter-of-factly. He didn't mince words. Brookside did not have a great reputation, he told them. Not within the neighborhood or within the city. "It's not a school with a lot of respect. It's not a place where educators want to come to teach," he said.

The teachers seemed taken aback. Maybe they were too close to the situation, too isolated in their own classrooms, Mr. Hay thought, to see how outsiders perceived the school. It was largely a veteran staff; many had been there for years. He continued. "What I can't understand, looking at the scores, is why this building has very few kids achieving at the highest level." The room fell silent. Finally, one teacher spoke up. "Well, these kids struggle at learning. They really can't go to that level," she said.

"I disagree," he replied, adding, "And we're going to change that."

Over the next forty minutes, Mr. Hay laid out his teaching philosophy, the one he'd had such success with in Massachusetts: Students would rise to whatever level they were asked to achieve. Set the bar low, he said, and improvement would be incremental, even for the best students. Set it high, and they'd make much greater leaps—even those at the bottom of the ladder. Do a better job, he said. *Require* them to achieve. Otherwise in middle school and later, in high school, they'd be unable to compete. "Each year, we ask the children to improve by ten percent," he challenged the faculty. "Why shouldn't we ask teachers to improve ten percent, too?"

That caught the staff's attention. He would hold them accountable. Mr. Hay pushed them to take risks in the classroom, to experiment with new teaching strategies and not worry if some failed. "When you find something that does work, share it with your colleagues," he urged. That was a new one for Mrs. Keefe, who, in her first year at Brookside, in 1997, had felt that the administration had created an atmosphere in which teachers were pitted against one another.

"When I started and CMT time came around," she recalled. "I asked the two other fifth-grade teachers, 'What should I be doing?' And they said, 'Getting them ready for the tests.'

"'I don't know what they're supposed to know,' I told them.

"The teachers said, 'We're not sure, either.' Well, between them, they probably had fifty years of experience. They didn't want to share. When I confronted one of them, she said, 'It's better that you learn to stand on your own two feet.'"

There weren't many questions for Mr. Hay when he finished. He had seemed to the staff like a nice enough guy, but who could tell? The new principal, concerned his message had left the teachers a little shell-shocked, tried to reassure them. "Things didn't get this way overnight, and they're not going to change overnight," he said. He encouraged the teachers to smile more, around the students and each other. "We're just going to work together and do the best we can."

"I thought that was the best thing he could say," Mrs. Keefe said.

The first curriculum change Mr. Hay attempted was with language arts. That fall, in 2003, the district had implemented a new elementary school reading series, published by the company now known as Houghton Mifflin Harcourt. The fifth-grade text was what educators call a basal reader—an anthology of short stories crafted not as children's literature but to teach specific reading skills that served as a one-size-fits-all lesson book, covering everything from plot and character development to theme to vocabulary to grammar. Teachers were issued an accompanying instructional guide that was tightly scripted, easy to master, and required little training.

Mr. Hay was not surprised by the district's choice of texts. Basal readers have been employed in American schools since the

1860s, the most famous of which were Scott Foresman and Company's Dick and Jane books. By 2003, though, in many school districts the format had fallen from favor. Dick and Jane–type stories weren't the kind, he said, that made a child run to the library, eager to read. Further, research showed that basal texts were poorly suited to advanced students, who often felt unchallenged by the content, while the weaker ones had trouble keeping up and grew easily frustrated. They best served the average achiever—a classification in shorter supply at Brookside than in most schools, even in Norwalk. "We were failing. We ranked eleventh or twelfth [among the twelve elementary schools] in the city," Mr. Hay said. "Within months, we recognized that the new curriculum wasn't working."

Mr. Hay decided to take a chance. A strong Norwalk principal, he had learned, could operate a school with unusual independence, the reason being that Dr. Corda, the superintendent, was perpetually preoccupied. Every month, it seemed, he was embroiled in a new, energy-sapping battle with the school board over staffing issues and the threat of a reduced budget. In that regard, little in the community had changed since colonial days. That freed Mr. Hay to act on his own. In addition to the Harcourt series, he implemented the Collins Writing Program, a teaching strategy he'd had success with in Massachusetts. Devised by a former Massachusetts educator, it emphasized the components of good writing, particularly expository writing, a primary focus of the CMT. The Collins system had been adopted by a number of U.S. schools. Mr. Hay purchased the program, including extensive professional training, with $1,500 of the school's Title I money. One of his goals was to bring a sense of continuity regarding how writing was taught at

Brookside. Till then, each teacher had been on his or her own. But the program never took off. The faculty didn't buy into it; some bridled at changing their established teaching styles, others felt it siphoned class time from the reading and comprehension issues they believed were at the core of their students' depressed CMT scores, which continued to crater.

The staff, still not entirely trusting, waited to see how Mr. Hay would respond. Without hesitation, he jettisoned the Collins program and kept moving forward, searching for strategies that would work. Over the next year, Mr. Hay trotted out dozens of ideas, big and small, trying to alter the personality of the school. He brought in a *MythBusters*-like scientist to teach students about light and sound. He met with the PTO, still populated and run almost entirely by minority white parents, and told them that in the future, the school assemblies they sponsored should reflect Brookside's student population. He then hired Hispanic entertainers to perform native songs and dances at an ethnic pride assembly. He convinced the Norwalk mayor and the local state senator and U.S. congressman to visit classrooms and read to the children. He made it clear to the staff that he would back them should any have a dispute with students, their parents, another staff member, or the district office. Still, by the end of the year, little had changed. Few classroom doors had opened. The faculty wars were slow to abate. Through subtle strategy, Mr. Hay tried to maneuver the staff into working together. "In meetings," Mr. Morey said, "he didn't tell teachers what to do. He told us what had to be done. He'd say, 'We need to form a math curriculum committee. Who's going to step up?'" Initially, there were few volunteers.

Mr. Hay found it equally difficult selling his vision of Brookside to the local community. The first few years of his tenure, a small but steady stream of parents whose children were among Brookside's highest achievers visited his office to ask why they shouldn't transfer their child to a better school. Mr. Hay didn't really have an answer. One of his primary jobs, he realized, was to recast the school's image. Though the private Mr. Hay shunned attention, he began to market his public self in a very different way. He sought out the local media. He phoned the *Norwalk Hour*'s education reporter at the slightest hint of good news—the purchase of a new set of classroom computers, an award won by one of his teachers—anything to put Brookside in a positive light. Parents of prospective new students, expecting a five-minute meet and greet, received an hour-long guided tour of the school. "Come with me," he'd say, during the construction period, and he'd escort a young couple into a classroom in the kindergarten wing, where the teacher was explaining the different sounds associated with the alphabet. He'd whisk them to a closed-off hallway and describe the computer room and new library being built. And then to the gymnasium site, where students, he said, would display their science fair projects, and to the music room, where they rehearsed for the Christmas *Nutcracker* concert. And finally, he would lead them toward the hallway that would house the new upper-grades wing. Along the way, he'd point out the classwork mounted on the walls, and tell the parents how far along their child would be by the time he reported to Mr. Morey's or Mrs. Keefe's or Mrs. Freeman's room. To visitors, he seemed more the mayor of Brookside than its principal.

The school year ended. The construction project was finally complete. The fourth and fifth graders and their teachers returned to a brighter, cheerier-looking main building. That, alone, lifted spirits. The library—"the hub of the school," Mr. Hay liked to say—moved to a space more than double its previous size, making it the largest of all Norwalk elementary school libraries, big enough to accommodate an expanded collection of fifteen thousand titles.

Those two years of going without a library had been difficult for the students. "The kids would come to me and say, 'When is the library going to open again? When are we going to have a library?'" Mrs. Madden recalled. "There are a lot of kids here who don't have the opportunity to go to the public library—their parents are working, or they don't have cars or money to purchase books at a bookstore—so all they had was what was in the teachers' classrooms."

When the library reopened, Mr. Hay encouraged Mrs. Madden to prune several thousand titles left over from the 1950s and 1960s ("I had books on the shelves that cost thirty-five cents," she said), and replace them with contemporary children's literature that better reflected Brookside's cultural makeup. "That's going to cost money," she said. One day Mr. Hay, who was seldom without a book of his own to read, approached the peppy, middle-aged librarian at her desk. "You and me and Mrs. Schaefer are going for a ride," he announced. A few days later the three drove an hour to the Scholastic Company's Danbury, Connecticut, warehouse, during one of the company's twice-a-year school sales, grabbed shopping carts, and went on a book-buying spree. Biographies, science fiction, girls' books, sports, picture books, serial fiction. They purchased about $1,500's worth of books, for which they paid $500, which was still a lot of money for a failing school enduring a budget cut. "I knew he had a rainy-day fund, but I never asked where it came from," Mrs. Madden said. "I just knew the library was important to him."

And yet, despite all he tried, the academic needle barely moved. The following year, 2005–06, just 64 percent of the school's fifth graders, 60 percent of its fourth graders, and 59 percent of its third graders tested proficient in reading on the CMT, and Brookside was labeled a school "in need of improvement." In U.S. Department of Education–speak, that was the equivalent of a dire warning. The state demanded a district improvement plan. The district, in turn, ordered each school to produce a plan of its own. At Brookside, and in all of Norwalk, where the entire system was deemed failing, an urgency filled the air. Mr. Hay's job seemed safe, but without better CMT scores, one could never be sure. Like the manager of an underachieving baseball team, the principal of a chronically failing school can survive only so long. Mr. Hay approached Mrs. Schaefer, long a proponent of experimentation, of change, and asked her to research other reading strategies Brookside might try.

Mrs. Schaefer, no fan of basal readers, was happy to do so. She had tried to alter the school's teaching strategy once before. Fifteen years earlier, while teaching third grade at Brookside, she had sought and received permission from one of Mr. Hay's predecessors to junk the language arts text she and the other third-grade teachers had been using and pilot a children's literature–based curriculum of her own. Mrs. Schaefer had discovered an unusual Harcourt text peppered with short fiction featuring characters and themes that more accurately reflected the students' everyday lives. There were children of color. Children with Hispanic first names. Stories that dealt with jealousy and loneliness and the petty arguments that separated friends. She'd found surprising success with it. It was still a one-size-fits-all text, and not every student had been able to read at the level the material required. But the majority of her students had been enthralled by the stories, to the point at which they'd been eager to check out books from the library. Mrs. Schaefer had not seen such enthusiasm in her students before. She grew curious about other cutting-edge reading programs out there. With the principal's permission, she began visiting area elementary schools, sitting in on language arts classes, picking the brain of every innovative reading teacher she could find. Her interest grew more acute when, with Mr. Hay's arrival in 2003, she was appointed a full-time literacy specialist. It struck her she was now responsible for literacy at a school where nearly 40 percent of the students were insufficiently literate. The task she faced was overwhelming.

To Mrs. Schaefer, there was no mystery as to why the number of poor readers was so high. More than a quarter of the students qualified as ESL learners. Many of their parents spoke English poorly or not at all, and were incapable of reading with their children or helping them with their fluency or comprehension skills. Many more, she said—not just those of the ESL children—were not book readers, and had no home libraries to speak of, nor did they purchase newspapers or magazines. One result was that Brookside students in general had an underdeveloped nonfiction vocabulary; it showed clearly on the CMT, which placed great emphasis on nonfiction comprehension skills. In addition, many parents did not carefully oversee their children's homework. "I ask students all the time," Mrs. Schaefer said, "'Do your parents check to see if you've finished your thirty minutes of reading?' And they say, 'No, I just tell them I did.'"

Mrs. Schaefer suspected that was the case with Marbella. She was right. There were no bookcases in Marbella's home. No news magazines lying around on the kitchen or coffee tables. (Although Marbella did keep several Justin Bieber fan magazines in her bedroom.) Mr. Morey had been crystal clear from the first day of school that everyone in the class was to read half an hour per night. Marbella, when pressed by a friend one afternoon in the presence of her mother, had admitted she often quit after fifteen minutes or less. Marbella's mother was disappointed but not surprised. Since returning to adult high school classes herself, to earn her degree, she had been trying to set a good example for her daughter. She had purchased three dictionaries. Learn, she told her daughter, from my mistakes. "I told Marbella," she said, "I was not a big reader when I was your age, but now that I'm getting older I feel like I need it. Even Daddy at his landscaping office, sometimes he doesn't understand a certain thing, and who does he call? Me. It's pushing me more to read. And you need to read, too." Her mother had paused. "So what do you think?" Marbella had shrugged. "Maybe I ought to meet with Mr. Morey or Mrs. Schaefer and see what reading level you are, and what books you should get at that level," her mother had said. Marbella had shrugged again.

Marbella's mother thought the main reason her daughter didn't like to read, at home or in class, was that she was more interested in being social. She'd look out the upstairs window from her study alcove, see the neighborhood kids riding their bikes, and want to play outside. Or she'd hear Aajah or one of her other classmates whispering in class and want to know what was going on.

To Mrs. Schaefer, it sounded as logical an explanation as any. In her experience, there were a dozen reasons why students didn't work hard, didn't achieve. Some were distracted by sports, some by falling in love for the first time, others by hunger or poverty or the death of a beloved family member. A few lacked confidence and simply stopped trying. But unlike some of the staff, Mrs. Schaefer did not limit blame to the students and their parents. A handful of Brookside teachers were—there was no other word for it, she said—boring. They made it difficult for students already facing a variety of learning challenges to get excited about reading. A high school or college student, she said, was mature enough to dislike a teacher and yet still learn from her; but an elementary school student's relationship with a teacher was far different. It was more elemental, more emotional. The two were together the entire day, as much like aunt and niece as teacher and student. Marbella had stalled in fourth grade in part because she didn't enjoy her teacher. Mrs. Schaefer, for all her doubts about Marbella, was somewhat sympathetic. She had on occasion sought out the woman, who was in her third year of teaching, to coach her on the need to develop a better relationship with her students. It hadn't seemed to help. "I told her, before you can teach kids anything, you have to form a relationship with every one of those kids in your classroom," Mrs. Schaefer said. "They have to know you care. And if you don't have that, if you don't establish community, they're not going to buy into your teaching."

The language arts program Mrs. Schaefer ultimately had recommended to Mr. Hay required an especially strong relationship between teacher and student. Called the Reading and Writing Project, it was conceived by Lucy Calkins, the Richard Robinson Professor of Children's Literature at Columbia University's Teachers College. Mrs. Schaefer had first heard of the program through a colleague at a neighboring Westport, Connecticut, elementary school. In theory and methodology, it couldn't have differed more from the way a basal reader was taught. Calkins believed that reading and writing skills were inextricably linked and that students learned them best through literature pegged to their individual reading level that they had self-selected. In other words, through a book they truly wanted to read. A class of twenty-one might use twenty-one separate titles as their texts.

Calkins's Reading and Writing Project was not a curriculum; it was a teaching strategy. Her idea was to run a language arts class in the form of a workshop, with the teacher operating more in the style of a mentor than an instructor. At the start of a one-hour period, the teacher would deliver a seven-to-twelve-minute mini-lesson on one specific topic, such as character development or theme. Often, particularly in the lower grades, she would conduct it in an intimate setting, gathering the students on a rug in the front of the classroom. Afterward, she would send the students back to their seats, where they would open their selected titles and read.

At Brookside, books were readily available to all students. Each classroom housed a library of well over one hundred titles, representing a wide spectrum of reading levels and genres. Students would "check out" a book, and after finishing, return it and select a new one. They learned to choose books suited to their reading ability—ones challenging enough to test their vocabulary two or three times per page but not so daunting that they'd grow discouraged and stop reading or so easy that they'd grow bored and do the same. Calkins called these "just-right books." Over the course of the school year, as a student's reading level rose, so would the sophistication of the just-right book he selected. That was the theory, anyway. There was always the danger that with too little oversight, students would pick whatever title their friend was reading.

The students would read silently for half an hour or so. During that time, the teacher would move from one student to the next, asking each, for example, a probing question designed to make them think how, as a result of a plot twist, a key character had changed. This meant the teacher had to be familiar with every book in her library. Afterward, the students would turn to a seatmate and each would describe to the other what they had read. One of Calkins's theories was that verbalizing helped clarify a student's thinking, making it easier to write about what he'd read. Near the end of the hour, the teacher would gather the children again on the rug, to reiterate the mini-lesson or to address a common reading or comprehension issue she had encountered while circulating around the room. Over the next hour she would conduct a fresh workshop, this time guiding students on their writing skills.

The first time Mrs. Schaefer saw Calkins's workshop model in action was in 2003, during Mr. Hay's first year at Brookside. One morning, with his permission, she drove to Stillmeadow Elementary School, in Stamford, Connecticut, to observe a first-grade class whose teacher had adopted the program. She brought along Mrs. Masone and Mrs. Gilroy, two first-grade teachers who shared Mrs. Schaefer's interest in researching new teaching techniques.

Mrs. Masone had been particularly eager to visit Stillmeadow. Four years earlier, she had been teaching fifth grade at Brookside.

One of her students had been a ten-year-old Mexican immigrant who had never been to school and could not read. Fifth-grade teachers are not trained to teach nonreaders, as first-grade teachers are. Mrs. Masone realized she had no idea how to teach the student basic, building-block skills, such as letter recognition and letter sounds. She sought out one of the school's veteran first-grade teachers and asked if she could sit in on one of her reading lessons. The process fascinated her. She returned to the teacher's classroom again and again. That summer, the teacher retired and Mrs. Masone requested to take her place. "I was fascinated by teaching reading," Mrs. Masone—who later earned a doctorate and became Brookside's assistant principal—recalled. Thirty-six, she has two young daughters of her own. "I just was absolutely hooked. I mean, the look on a kid's face when he actually can read a word, there's nothing better than that. It's like a drug. Even today, I can't get enough of listening to kids read."

Together, the Brookside visitors took seats in the back of the classroom and, like theatergoers, watched the Stillmeadow teacher conduct her lesson. The day's topic was how to read with a partner.

"Watch me, and I'll show you how to sit," the teacher said to the class. She pointed to one of her students and asked, "Will you be my partner?"

The child walked to where the teacher was standing, and then the two sat, knees to knees, on an area rug. The teacher took the book the child was holding. "I'll read a page, and then you'll read a page, and we'll go back and forth and talk about what the book's about," she said. The rest of the class gathered on the rug, wrapped in a horseshoe around them.

The two read to one another, like actors trading lines. None of the Brookside teachers recall the title of the book. But they were struck by the teacher's method, and how it encouraged the student to focus, to assimilate, to think. Perhaps the teacher had selected a precocious student, they thought. But then the teacher announced it was time for everyone to read, and the students split into preassigned pairs, based on reading ability. They grabbed their just-right books, found spots on the floor and plopped down knee to knee.

Most impressive was that the students did precisely as their teacher asked. Many read with a facility that exceeded Brookside's first graders. Moreover, in large part they maintained their focus, even as the teacher spent private time with students on the opposite side of the room. Over the course of the next thirty minutes, she listened to each pair as they read aloud, some from remedial books, others from titles more advanced. Sometimes, to help lead them in the right direction with comprehension, she asked questions of her own. "You could see they were engaged," Mrs. Schaefer recalled, "and it was because they liked what they were reading."

Back at Brookside, Mrs. Schaefer spent time in Mrs. Masone's and Mrs. Gilroy's classrooms, trying to replicate for their students what the three of them had witnessed at Stillmeadow. It proved difficult. All they had to go by were their one-time observations and the little workshop material Mrs. Schaefer had read. "I tried it in my room, and it was a disaster at the beginning," Mrs. Masone recalled. "The kids didn't know where to sit. They were rolling on the floor. I found out it's a very challenging way of teaching. You have to be at the top of your game to teach the model well." Mrs. Schaefer, widely considered among the most skilled in the district at teaching children to read, convinced Mr. Hay to send her to Teachers College over the summer, to immerse herself in Calkins's program.

When Mrs. Schaefer reported back that Brookside should adopt the program, Mr. Hay had a decision to make. Investing in it would be no cheap date. The initial outlay—roughly $30,000 for both faculty training and follow-up coaching by Teachers College consultants ("so, as the staff was going along and finding bumps in the road," Mr. Hay said, "they would have an opportunity to talk to somebody")—would represent almost one fourth of Brookside's $140,000 in annual Title I funding. And that didn't take into account the expense of the hundred or more just-right books each of the fifteen first- through fifth-grade teachers would require to stock their classroom libraries.

For Mr. Hay, it represented a tremendous gamble. No Norwalk school employed the workshop model. The district would not help bankroll it. He was on his own. In the end, he felt he had no choice. "Maybe if we were a school in [a wealthy community like] Darien, where many of the students are high achievers, we wouldn't need a program designed for so much diversity," he said. "But we are who we are, and we had to do something. Our scores couldn't get any lower." Because first grade was the critical grade for teaching reading and because Brookside's first-grade teachers were, perhaps more than the other teachers, open to change, Mr. Hay and Mrs. Schaefer decided to pilot the program there. The second year, they rolled it out to the fifth grade and then to the rest of the school.

"There was grumbling at first," Mr. Hay recalled. "Anything new takes a while to be accepted." This was his diplomatic way of saying that the school's veteran teachers, having developed an entrenched teaching routine, had little stomach for starting over with an entirely new system. Some teachers dragged their feet, teaching the workshop model only when Mr. Hay or Mrs. Schaefer dropped in to observe them. Others taught it but not with the commitment required to teach it well. That may explain why, initially, Brookside's language arts CMT scores showed little improvement. Mr. Hay, though, was persistent. Each summer he paid for several teachers to attend an intensive, one-week training session at Teachers College. Invariably, they returned as converts. In the teacher's lounge, they functioned as his Johnny Appleseeds, spreading the wisdom of the workshop model to their colleagues.

It wasn't until the 2007–08 school year, by which time Calkins's program was firmly embedded at Brookside, that scores began to improve. That year, reading proficiency among fifth graders jumped 13 percent, to 80.7 percent. The fourth graders improved by 10 percent, to 61.7 percent. The students made a similar leap in math. Two years earlier, Brookside had been on the state's watch list as a school "in need of improvement." Now it had earned placement in the category known as "safe harbor." The school was still failing, but overall, its students had made significant progress.

In 2008–09, Marbella and Hydea's class entered third grade, meaning they were subject to CMT testing for the first time. Mr. Hay and Mrs. Schaefer had been concerned about this group from the start; relative to Brookside's other students, they seemed less advanced. The CMT bore this out. Just 57.4 were judged proficient in reading, a dip of 6 percent from what the previous third-grader class had scored. In math, the drop-off was less severe; 77.9 percent reached proficiency, as opposed to 80.6 percent of third graders from the year before.

The school administrators had gone to great pains to identify those areas in which the girls' class had performed the weakest on the exams. Two had stood out: vocabulary and basic math facts, especially multiplication and division. The following year—Marbella and Hydea's fourth-grade year—extra time had been carved from the curriculum schedule, enabling their teacher to focus more on those areas. Mr. Hay had heard of a wonderful, on-line tutorial program called Study Island that taught vocabulary and math facts—and every other major subject—in an engaging, game-like interactive manner. He had urged the faculty to make use of it during the school day, and for once they had. That spring, the grade's CMT scores improved. A total of 65.6 percent demonstrated proficiency in reading, while 83.6 percent reached that level in math. Now as fifth graders, Mr. Hay hoped they'd boost their scores still higher. Even if they did, though, he knew it probably wouldn't be enough for the school to escape its failing status.

The trouble, Mr. Hay said, was that the pass/fail line was an ever-moving target. In the national race to 100 percent proficiency that NCLB demanded by 2014, Connecticut, like every state, was playing catch up. Every two years, according to the timetable the state legislature had set, the bar for compliance—the percentage of students required to be proficient in language arts and math (and for fifth graders, beginning in 2011, science)—increased by roughly 10 percent. In 2011, that number would rise to about 89 percent. "There's almost no way we reach that," Mr. Hay said. "Our kids are improving, but No Child Left Behind doesn't give credit for improvement [for students still short of grade level]. It's all or nothing with them."

That September, a weird dichotomy swept the school. The

teachers, Mr. Morey included, careened from downplaying the importance of the coming CMT to issuing their students tough-love warnings. "Safe harbor" seemed anything but safe. Seated at his desk one afternoon, Mr. Morey watched with dismay as his students quickly lost focus during twenty minutes of independent reading. First, Carlos raised his hand and asked to go to the bathroom. "You're going to have to wait," Mr. Morey said. After five minutes, Dennis checked the clock, to see how much longer he'd have to read. A minute later, Kyle rose from his seat and walked to the sink. "I have to wash Magic Marker from my finger," he explained. After nine minutes, Sergio got up for a drink of water. Carlos followed. "Why are you drinking? I thought you had to go to the bathroom," Mr. Morey asked. "My throat's dry," Carlos answered. At the ten-minute mark, Sara yawned and Dennis fidgeted.

Mr. Morey had had enough. "I'm asking you to read quietly for twenty minutes," he admonished the class, rising from his seat. "On the CMT, you have to focus for an hour." The students hushed and returned to their books. It was the reaction Mr. Morey had hoped for, but he wasn't sure instilling fear of the CMT was an appropriate message, especially this early in the school year. He shook his head, sat back down, tried to come up with a better strategy. He soon needed one. Within minutes, several students had resumed whispering or daydreaming or playing with their pencil erasers. The CMTs were in March, six months distant—to them, a lifetime away.

Chapter 3

October 2010

The phone rang at 4:25 P.M., forty-five minutes after Marbella arrived home from school, twenty minutes after she finished her fruit and juice snack. Aajah was on the line. "Are you doing your homework?" she asked. "I need help with math." Since fourth grade, the two had talked almost daily after school by telephone. The phone was central to their best friendship, as they rarely saw one another away from Brookside. In all their time together, they had never shared a sleepover, never had a playdate, never visited the other's home. Well, that was not entirely accurate. Once, Aajah said, she had stopped on the sidewalk outside Marbella's house. She had spotted Marbella in an upstairs window, but her friend had not come down. They had talked of getting together—with Hydea, too—but for some reason it had not yet worked out.

The two chitchatted about class for several minutes—how Mr.

Morey had unloaded on Fernando that day for not paying attention (Marbella had liked that; she had no love for Fernando, who
often made faces at her and sometimes stuck out his tongue when
he caught her eye), the horrible-looking string beans served at
lunch, how mean Mrs. Bernstein, the music teacher, had yelled at
the entire fifth grade for not knowing the lyrics to "The Christmas
Tree Feud," one of the holiday songs they'd be performing in December at the Norwalk Senior Center. Marbella tried to dish about
Justin Bieber—she just wanted to die every time she heard his hit
"Somebody to Love"—but Aajah wouldn't bite. Aajah had maxed
out on Bieber—she'd rather listen to Marbella and Hydea sing, she
said—and steered the conversation back to Mrs. Bernstein. Then
the two got down to business. Mr. Morey had given them a simple
long division problem in class: $3\overline{)390}$. A number of the students,
including Aajah, were unable to solve it. But instead of wrestling
with the problem, Aajah had given up and started whispering to
Carlos, seated beside her. Mr. Morey had jumped all over her.
"You can't learn division by gabbing away and then saying, 'I don't
get it,'" he had barked, before turning to the rest of the class. "Boys
and girls," he told them, "we've been doing these same kind of
problems every day, and if I didn't care about you goofing off, I'd
let you get away with it. But I do care. How can you learn when
you talk to the person next to you?"

Aajah had wanted to apologize. She didn't, because fifth-grade
protocol called for her to simply lower her head. The thing was, she
liked Mr. Morey. He made things fun. His respect meant a lot to
her. Worse, now he and everybody else knew that she—one of a
dozen fifth graders designated academically talented—had trouble
with math. Aajah was embarrassed. Marbella wasn't great at math,

either, but she was better at it than Aajah. Mr. Morey had assigned the class twenty long division problems for homework, and Aajah needed her help. "It's like, I'm better than Marbella at writing, so she calls me whenever we have to write something for homework," Aajah said. She could have gone to one of her three older brothers for help, just as Marbella could have sought aid from her three older sisters. But older siblings weren't like best friends. The two spoke for almost an hour.

That day, Hydea had struggled with long division, too. Like Aajah, she had given up in the middle of trying to solve a problem: $4\overline{)560}$. Mr. Morey didn't suspect, though, because she had sat at her desk quiet as a mouse. There had been a moment when she had considered approaching him for help, but she had decided against it. She was too shy, and besides, she worried that if she sought his assistance, the others would think her dumb. Just that week, she had raised her hand to answer a question on decimals, and though she'd gotten it wrong, she had almost been right. Still, she could hear Carlos sniggering at her.

Hydea figured she'd call Aajah when she got home and maybe work on their homework together. But that afternoon, she kept getting a busy signal. Lately, Aajah's line had often been busy. Talking with Marbella, she assumed. She didn't want to feel jealous, but it was hard not to. She didn't like Marbella monopolizing her closest friend. Hydea didn't have many other classmates with whom she felt close. There had been Jasmine, a girl in Mrs. Bohrer's class, but their friendship had cooled since fourth grade, when Hydea began to spend most of her time with Aajah and Marbella. She could ask her older sister, Billi, but Billi had her own busy life. That left Grandma. She was always available to help, but she didn't always teach the same way as Mr. Morey, and often in class the next day, Hydea would find she still didn't understand.

Oh well, Hydea thought. She got what assistance she could from Grandma, finished up, hopped on her bicycle and headed down the sidewalk. Maybe she would spot Marbella playing outside. She stopped on her side of the busy street, opposite Marbella's house. Marbella wasn't around. Even if she had been, it probably wouldn't have mattered, Hydea realized. Neither girl was permitted to cross the street on her own.

The next day Hydea squirmed in her seat when Mr. Morey asked the students to take out their math homework. "I want to go over your answers," he said. Hydea tried to make herself invisible, but that was difficult, being the tallest girl in the room. Aajah, who was tall, too, and whose flowery outfits and ever-changing hairstyles made her somewhat distinctive, was nervous as well. They both wished they could be more like Marbella, who seemed less stressed when called on and unaffected if she answered wrong.

"Maybe," Mr. Morey said to the class, in a voice much quieter than the one he had used the previous day, "the problem is that you didn't understand the question." He picked up a brown marker and wrote on the whiteboard: $4\overline{)560}$. "Think of it like this," he said, turning to the students. "You just won a prize of five hundred sixty dollars and you want to split it equally among your four best friends. How much do you give to each?" The students nodded; they understood the concept. Still, about a quarter were unable to solve the problem. "How many times does four go into five?" he asked. *It's like pulling teeth*, he thought.

When Mr. Morey had first decided to be a teacher, he had

never imagined the patience it would require. Like Mr. Hay, his childhood dreams had not included standing in front of a classroom of ten-year-olds. For years, he'd had no firm idea what he wanted to do. He had been a good high school baseball player—good enough to make the all-county team as a second baseman but not quite skilled enough to earn a college athletic scholarship, let alone play professionally. He had encountered a similar problem with basketball. After high school, he had enlisted in the U.S. Air Force, putting off college for a while. He'd looked on it not only as a stopgap, but as a family right of passage; his father had joined the air force and his grandfather had fought in World War II. Mr. Morey had figured he'd serve a few years and sort things out. Through good fortune he had been stationed at Hickam Air Force Base, in Hawaii. He had loved it there. He wasn't in a war zone, and the weather was great. But after three and a half years, he still had felt at loose ends. With vague plans to eventually attend college, he had mustered out. Returning home, he found work at an electronics firm but didn't like it very much. He took a few classes at Dutchess Community College, about thirty miles from where he had lived in high school but felt no urge to register for more. "I was wide open. I had no career goal," he said.

Partly to stay physically active, partly to hang with his friends, Mr. Morey joined a local, recreation-league doubles volleyball team. One night by chance, the volleyball coach at the State University of New York at New Paltz saw him play. "If you ever decide to go to school," the coach told him, "give me a call." Several months later, the electronics company where Mr. Morey worked went out of business. Reduced to working part-time delivering pizza, he contacted the New Paltz coach. That fall, he entered the school as a full-time student and player on the volleyball and basketball teams. Mr. Morey, a freshman, was twenty-three years old.

For a while, he thought he would study to be a physical therapist. But New Paltz did not offer a four-year sports medicine program, meaning he would have to transfer to another school to get his degree. He switched his major to communications, a field that held no particular interest for him. After graduating, Mr. Morey stayed around campus, working part-time as an assistant basketball coach and part-time for a program that helped international students land job internships. "I knew I couldn't stay there forever," he said. "I wasn't making a whole lot of money." He toyed with going to law school. But then a friend of a friend told him about an internship for would-be schoolteachers at the University of Bridgeport, in Connecticut. "He said it was a year long, and you do student teaching, and in a year and a half you're a teacher," Mr. Morey said. "Law school meant another three years of school. I was twenty-nine. I was like, I don't want to wait another three years before I'm working."

He enrolled and whisked through the program. He had wanted to teach middle school math, but gave it up after discovering it required additional credits. Not wanting to wait any longer for his teaching certificate, he opted for a general degree instead. He left school qualified solely as an elementary school teacher. Mr. Morey still had no real hunger for the job. His goal had been to land steady work in a solid, job-protected profession.

That changed when he began his internship at Redding (Connecticut) Elementary School. He worked with children in four grades, from first through fourth. What he found was that teaching was like coaching sports. He could spend his days bringing out the best in young people. He could instill in them an eagerness to learn. And he could see the product of his work not just on their test scores but in the way they blossomed as people, as they acquired knowledge and skills. It was there in their eyes.

Mr. Morey found work quickly after graduation, first teaching summer reading at Tracey Elementary School, in Norwalk, and then at Brookside. It was his fortune, he felt, to be the rare man seeking an elementary school job. "If I was a woman," he acknowledged, "I probably would have been a dime a dozen." When he arrived at Brookside, he was thirty-two years old.

From the start, Mr. Morey was extraordinarily happy in his job, especially after Mr. Hay's arrival. But eventually, like many male elementary school teachers, his thoughts turned to heading his own school. He enrolled in a University of Bridgeport nighttime program that led to a master's degree in education administration. To his surprise, he didn't like it. "What I realized," he said, "was that my heart was in teaching. All I wanted was to be a classroom teacher." He left the master's program and has never looked back.

The morning after his unsuccessful long division lesson, Mr. Morey had arrived at school early. He sat at his desk, idly scrolling through his e-mail. He couldn't quite figure out his class. It was different, he thought, from most of his previous groups. He had always taught a wide range of achievers. But almost all his past classes had had two or three extraordinarily bright, hardworking students whose leadership helped lift how the others performed. This class had several smart children—Josh and Jacky and Kyle— but none who possessed that special charisma he was looking for.

He thought back to a library session a few days earlier. The children were studying the early Western Hemisphere explorers, and he had assigned to each an expedition leader to research. He had expected to do some hand holding; after all, he was dealing with ten-year-olds. With the help of Mrs. Madden, he had procured them books and suggested relevant websites. All had commenced to read. All but Carlos, who had immediately raised his hand.

"Can you help me?" he had asked Mr. Morey.

"Carlos, you haven't even tried yet. How do you know you need help?"

"Please. Just help me," he had said.

Mr. Morey had tried to hide his exasperation. "Carlos, come here," he had said. The boy shuffled to where Mr. Morey was seated. "Tell me," the teacher had asked, "What responsibilities do you have at home?"

"What?" Carlos had asked, thrown by the question.

"Responsibilities. What chores do you have?"

He had shrugged. "I don't do any."

"Well, starting tomorrow, you will," Mr. Morey had said. "I'm going to talk to your parents, and I'm going to tell them to give you chores. And they're going to be tied to sports. If you don't do your chores, you won't be able to play sports. You're not going to like it. You're not going to like me. I'm not doing it to punish you. Having chores will give you responsibility and make you a better person, and I can live with that."

Carlos had returned to his seat looking confused, trying to figure out what had just happened. The exchange had made Mr. Morey curious. He motioned to Josh, his best student. "What are your responsibilities at home?" he had asked. "I have to do the dishes and sometimes clean my room," the boy had replied. In turn, Mr. Morey had queried Dennis, Jacky, Hydea, and Marbella. Dennis, like Carlos, had no chores. Jacky made her bed, helped with the laundry, and cleaned her room. Hydea did the same. Marbella had chores but had to be bribed to do them. He sent them back to their seats. "Notice any correlation between chores and those who take their schoolwork seriously?" he had said, rhetorically, to a teacher's aide sitting beside him. There were times, Mr. Morey thought, when it was the parents who needed a talking to.

Dr. Susan Marks, the new superintendent, had voiced quite a different take on this subject in her August introductory speech to the Norwalk faculty and staff: To her, blaming parents or other outside forces for students' failures was unacceptable. "We're here to do the job, no excuses," she had said. Personally, Mr. Morey thought that was a lot of hooey. But there it was. At least he knew, after the long division lesson and the library session, what he was up against. Somehow, he was going to have to find a way to reach the slackers in his class. If he could win just one of them over, one student who was popular, whom the children considered a leader, he might turn the class around.

The parents of two of Mr. Morey's students happened to stop by Brookside that very night. Mrs. Schaefer was hosting the first of four reading workshops she would conduct for parents over the course of the year. The idea was to offer tips to help improve their child's fluency and comprehension as they read together at home. Presuming that they read together at all.

That was no sure thing. Many of the school's 142 ESL students came from homes in which one or both parents were not literate in English. As many or more families, Mrs. Schaefer knew, operated on the honor system: The children told their parents they'd read for the required homework time (thirty minutes for the fifth graders) and their parents chose to believe them. Carlos and his mother were fairly typical. Carlos—a bright child who in fourth grade had tested poorly on the reading portion of the CMT—generally read in bed, before going to sleep. He didn't hide the fact that he didn't enjoy it; for him it involved too much quiet and lying around. "I have a stopwatch," he confided to a friend. "I'll read for, like, four minutes and then I'll take a break, and then I'll read another four minutes and take another break. Maybe three times a week I'll read for the whole thirty minutes and turn off the stopwatch. The other nights, like fifteen. My mom just checks on me once a night."

The last time Mrs. Schaefer had organized a similar reading night, in the spring of the previous school year, perhaps 25 parents had attended. On this evening, roughly 125 had gathered in Brookside's cafeteria. Mrs. Schaefer was smart enough to understand she wasn't the draw. The parents had come for the free cheese pizza and soft drinks, advertised on the flyer she and Mr. Hay had sent home with the students the day before. Mrs. Schaefer had hoped the free meal would attract the parents of Brookside's poorest-performing students. But the opposite had occurred. There were far more white parents in attendance than Hispanics, and far more Hispanics than blacks. Of the three groups, Brookside's black students had proved the weakest on the CMT. And yet, just three black students and their parents had come. Neither Mrs. Schaefer nor Mr. Hay could say why. Mrs. Schaefer had recognized two students from Mr. Morey's class. She spotted a shy boy named Leo, seated beside his Ecuadorian father. Leo's parents, she knew, were sincere about improving their son's reading. She had worked with Leo before. She was somewhat surprised to see another of Mr. Morey's students—a white girl who read at grade level and had always done well on the CMT. She was with her father, whom Mrs. Schaefer had never seen before. He had come, he confessed, because he'd had a fight with his wife and needed an excuse to leave the house.

After half an hour, the pizza boxes were cleared away and Mrs. Schaefer raised a microphone. She had waited long months for this moment, ever since July, when she had first eyed the school's failing 2010 language arts CMT scores. The staff and faculty, she had been certain, wouldn't be able to conquer the school's literacy problem alone. They would need help from the parents. This would be the night she'd win their support. She stepped to the front of the room.

"How many parents tell stories to their kids?" she asked. About two thirds raised their hand. "How many take your kids shopping with you?" she continued. Pretty much the same people responded. She paused, scanning the cafeteria. Mrs. Schaefer has a soft voice, and she had trouble projecting it, even with the help of a microphone. Already, parents were whispering to one another in the back of the room. Mrs. Schaefer tried to ignore them. She rattled off a series of fun, creative ways for parents to teach reading skills to their children. She suggested they sing songs with their kids, as a means of introducing them to rhythm and rhyme. At the supermarket, she recommended having their children read the names of items on the shelves. When at a restaurant, she said, youngsters should read the menu aloud. At home, while preparing dinner, Mom could request their help reading the recipe. "Reading," Mrs. Schaefer emphasized, "isn't limited to books." She paused. The murmuring grew louder. At her feet, a gaggle of schoolchildren chatted, making it even more difficult for people in the back to hear. She wondered how many parents were still listening. Not many, she suspected. But it was too late to alter her presentation. She soldiered on.

"I'm going to pick five or six of the children sitting here, and demonstrate what we call a read-around," she said. "It's very easy to do. I'm going to work with beginning readers, but you can try some of the same things with an older child, at home, as well."

Mrs. Schaefer set a basketball, a salt shaker and a pair of sneakers upon a folding table. The parents quieted somewhat, curious. She picked up a book and faced the children, who were seated in a horseshoe around her on the cafeteria floor. The book, *Salt in His Shoes*, was co-authored by Deloris Jordan and Roselyn Jordan, Michael Jordan's mother and sister, respectively. It told how Michael, through hard work and dedication, became a basketball icon.

"Who can tell me what this book is about?" she asked the students, before she started reading.

A first-grade girl raised her hand. "It's about basketball," she said, "because the boy on the cover is holding a basketball." Mrs. Schaefer enthusiastically agreed.

Salt in His Shoes is a picture book. Mrs. Schaefer went through it page by page, focusing solely on the pictures. One showed a little boy frowning. "What do you think the boy is feeling?" Mrs. Schaefer asked. With each picture, the story began to unfold for both the children and adults. "Before we even start reading," Mrs.

Schaefer explained to the parents, "the children have a good idea of what the book is about."

Mrs. Schaefer returned to the first page and began to read. In order to do so, though, she had to set down the microphone. One of the Hispanic parents moved closer, trying to hear. Each time Mrs. Schaefer came to a picture, she paused and asked the children to connect it to the text. It was the very heart of her lesson— with emerging readers, pictures make words recognizable, filling them with meaning. But few parents could catch what she was saying. Mrs. Schaefer's voice barely carried past the children at her feet. Across the room, fingers started dancing on the keyboards of smartphones. A group of parents in the center of the room turned their backs to Mrs. Schaefer and the students and began chatting. The undercurrent of talk grew louder. Mrs. Schaefer finished reading, and asked the children to retell and summarize the story. But their voices were small, and it was impossible to make out what they said. A husband and wife gathered their children and left. Others followed. Mrs. Schaefer, raising her voice, tried one last time to reach the audience, to hold them. "We prepared to read, we read the story, we talked about the story," she said in summary, as loud as she could. "It's the best way to get kids to learn."

Few heard her. By then, almost everyone was headed for the door. It was a missed opportunity.

Hydea was afraid of heights. The following day at recess, while Marbella and Aajah competed to see who could soar higher on the swings, Hydea remained in the equivalent of the slow lane, content to remain closer to the ground. Hydea wished she could be more like her two daredevil friends. They were fearless, she thought, Marbella in particular. In gym period, Marbella plowed past everybody, her twin pigtails flying—soccer, basketball, it didn't matter what the sport. Hydea couldn't imagine doing that. Her essential shyness just wouldn't allow her to let go. Her best sport was running, in which she competed entirely on her own.

It didn't seem fair to Hydea that her nature should work against her in the classroom, but on this day, it appeared to be the case. For several weeks, Mr. Morey had been making reference to the CMT. Now for the first time, he was getting serious. There was a portion of the writing skills exam called the open-ended question. It asked for students to read a short essay or expository story, and then write about it. Grammar, spelling, punctuation, and the like counted for some of the grade, but only a small portion. The primary skills it tested were organization, clarity of thought, and most important, the ability to extrapolate the main point of a piece and identify the key details the author cited in its support.

The sample open-ended question on this day concerned a Brooklyn-born Vietnam War veteran named Charlie DeLeo. For more than thirty years, first as a U.S. National Park Service employee and later, after his retirement, as a volunteer, DeLeo was known as the Keeper of the Flame. The flame he kept lit was the torch atop the Statue of Liberty. Over the years he climbed the statue more than twenty-five hundred times to change its light bulbs and to clean and help maintain it. According to the five-hundred-word story Mr. Morey distributed to Hydea and her classmates, DeLeo had weathered lightning strikes, injurious falls, and more in order to do his job. The question the students had to answer was this: Explain whether or not you would like a job such as Charlie DeLeo's. Use the information from the passage and from your own experience to support your answer.

Mr. Morey had been very clear about the format they were to follow in order to pass. They were to start, he said, by restating the question. He grabbed a marker and wrote on the whiteboard, *I would like/not like a job like Charlie DeLeo's because* . . . "Maybe you think his job is cool, because it's an adventure," Mr. Morey said, "or maybe it's the last job you'd want, because being up there is so scary." Next, he said, they were to cite an example pulled from the story that made their point. Following that, he said, they were to write a sentence or two relating their own experience to DeLeo's. "For example," Mr. Morey said. "Maybe you went to Playland [a nearby amusement park] and got scared going way up on the roller coaster, and you're afraid that climbing straight up a steel ladder into the torch would be just as scary." The next sentence, he said, would enumerate a second example from the story that supported their main point. Finally, they'd end by restating the question—again. *So, in conclusion, I would like/not like a job like Charlie DeLeo's because* . . . "If you follow that order exactly on the CMT," Mr. Morey said, "I guarantee you will pass."

Hydea felt overwhelmed. All that Mr. Morey had said—it was a lot to remember. And though he had emphasized there was no right or wrong answer, that what mattered was how well you made a case for wanting DeLeo's job or not, she worried that the author wouldn't have written about him in the first place unless his job was pretty cool. She didn't know where to start.

Hydea fiddled with her eraser. She glanced at Aajah, trying to catch her eye, but Aajah, her shoulders hunched forward, her head bent over her paper, was hard at work. She toyed with asking Mr. Morey for help but didn't feel comfortable approaching him. Hydea didn't know him well enough for that. She glanced at the clock. Ten minutes left. She had to write something. She pursed her lips, bent over the blank page and began writing. Even as she did, though, she knew she was not making much sense. Later, when she arrived home and her grandma asked how her day had been, she answered that things had gone okay. She felt bad enough on her own. She didn't want to upset her grandma, as well.

When Mr. Morey reviewed Hydea's paper, he was disappointed but not surprised. He knew, from talking to her about whatever just-right book she happened to be reading, that she had a pretty good notion of plot and theme, the tendencies of its main characters, where the action was headed. Her weakness, he thought, was organizing her thoughts on paper. More precisely, she had difficulty marshaling and connecting facts to produce the type of persuasive essay favored by the CMT. Too bad, Mr. Morey thought, because he saw real potential in Hydea. At the start of the year, he had told his students to keep a daily journal in which they could write about anything, and he'd read Hydea's entries—longer than most—which often contained flights of fancy about her make-believe land, Rabia. Given the freedom to compose a fictional story, to let loose her imagination, her talent had placed her nearer the head of the class.

Mr. Morey felt for Hydea. He wasn't a big fan of the writing template he was required to teach. Like her, his favorite school subject through college had been creative writing. There was nothing at all creative, he believed, about crafting a CMT-style open-ended response. Certainly, it emphasized important skills such as story structure and critical thinking. But to him, the format was little more than a paint-by-numbers memorization drill. What did restating a question at the start and finish of every piece, with the same three boilerplate paragraphs inserted in between, have to do with creative thinking, with the art of persuasive writing? How would his students learn that there is more than one way to tackle a problem? He shook his head. It was useless to harp on it. His job was to provide his students with the necessary skills to pass the CMT. That was the priority. Through Christmas vacation, he would still have freedom to craft his own language arts lessons. Come January, though, when CMT prep began in earnest, there would be little time for anything else. His thoughts returned to Hydea. In the last two months, she had shown herself to be a surprisingly dedicated student. By the end of the year, he thought, she had a chance to reach grade level in reading. He decided to consult Mrs. Schaefer.

Mrs. Schaefer had been thinking about Hydea, as well. She was curious to see how the ten-year-old was doing. She was still trying to decide between Hydea and Marbella for the final spot in her fifth-grade CMT prep tutorial group, set to begin January 2. At the moment, she was still leaning toward Marbella. Marbella was a bit more advanced with her fluency and comprehension, and though she seemed not to care much about improving her skills, she nevertheless always did as she was told. Hydea, Mrs. Schaefer worried, was so shy and lacking in confidence that she'd be difficult to reach and certainly would not ask for help.

Mr. Morey had a request. He wanted to enroll Hydea in another of Mrs. Schaefer's special-help programs. Wednesdays and Thursdays during the fall and winter semesters, Mrs. Bohrer and Mrs. Keefe ran hour-long, after-school workshops for twelve of the slower fifth-grade readers, under Mrs. Schaefer's direction. Admission to the groups was by invitation only. Mrs. Schaefer and the three fifth-grade teachers selected the students. To demonstrate their interest, the children had to present Mrs. Schaefer with a signed permission slip from their parents or guardians. She gave them two weeks to do it; those who missed the deadline risked losing their spot.

Mr. Morey recommended that she consider Hydea. With a little extra support, he said, Hydea might be ready to turn things around. Mrs. Schaefer was intrigued; she had been thinking the same thing. Though she had monitored Hydea since first grade, she had never invited the girl into one of her special programs.

Hydea had always lagged in reading comprehension and writing but never to the degree that required urgent attention. Instead, starting in first grade, the literacy specialist would visit her class and sometimes pull her aside for half an hour, along with two or three other struggling students, while her teacher worked with the rest of the children. At the time, Hydea had trouble recognizing what are called sight words—words such as *a*, *the*, *and*, and *is* that come up often in reading. A student who has mastered those words is free to concentrate on the more difficult parts of reading, such as comprehension. But Hydea had trouble making that elemental step. In second grade she improved, if incrementally, thanks to a daily, half-hour, before-school tutoring session with her teacher, Mrs. Roman.

Third grade found Hydea still behind. "She sat in the middle of the room, just trying to blend in," her teacher, Miss Sutton, recalled. "She didn't want to bring attention to herself. That would have killed her, if something happened and I singled her out. But she never did anything for me to single her out. She was a very sweet, but very timid girl, maybe because she was self-conscious about being the tallest in the class. If I asked her a question, and she didn't know the answer, her eyes would go blank. If she did know the answer, she'd speak so softly that I couldn't hear her. We had a classroom aide who worked with her a lot. If Hydea kept to her just-right book level, she didn't do too badly. But when it came to CMT prep, that was a whole different story. The CMT prep work was above her just-right level, and the prep period lasted a little more than two months. She struggled the entire time."

Hydea's fourth-grade year was her most difficult. Where before she had tried her best in class, that year she showed little effort. Part of the reason was social. She grew close to Aajah and Marbella, two extremely outgoing girls, and mimicked some of their devil-may-care behavior. But part was the fault of her relatively inexperienced teacher, who lacked charisma and had difficulty controlling the class. Over the course of the year, Hydea's reading progress stalled and even regressed. Mrs. Schaefer kept tabs on students through their CMT and reading level scores. For day-to-day matters, though, she depended on intel from their teachers. For some reason, Hydea's teacher never alerted Mrs. Schaefer about the girl's struggles till the end of the year, when she recommended Hydea for summer school.

"I had to test any student going to summer school," Mrs. Schaefer said. "That was when I really took a look at Hydea, and I was somewhat concerned about her because of her thinking process. She could read the words, but she really couldn't comprehend what she was reading as well as she should. I tested her in fourth grade before summer school, and I was shocked when she came out at level twenty-eight. A twenty-eight is the end of second grade."

Summer school helped Hydea. When Mrs. Schaefer retested her after the start of fifth grade, she had improved to Level 38, which translated to a beginning fourth-grade reader. She was still a year behind. But if what Mr. Morey had said was true, the ten-year-old had the potential to make significant and rapid progress.

The more Mrs. Schaefer considered Hydea, and Mr. Morey's enthusiasm for her, the more she was inclined to volunteer her help. The morning after her discussion with Mr. Morey, she stopped the fifth grader in the hallway and asked if she was interested in joining Mrs. Keefe's after-school reading group. Hydea was struck all but speechless. She had received extra help in reading in each of the last two summers, when she had attended summer school. But she had always looked upon summer classes as a punishment. This was the first time anyone had taken a special interest in her. "Um hmm," she answered, with a big smile. She took the permission slip, placed it carefully inside a book so it wouldn't get wrinkled, and returned the book to her backpack.

A week passed. No signed permission slip. Mrs. Schaefer went to Mr. Morey's class to investigate. Maybe, the literacy specialist thought, Hydea wasn't as motivated as she seemed. When she asked about the permission slip, Hydea ducked her head and said, apologetically, "I forgot." Mrs. Schaefer told her she'd give her till

Monday, and then left. Several minutes passed. While the rest of the class silently read their just-right books, Mr. Morey spied Hydea rummaging through her desk. He watched as she pulled free a crumpled piece of paper, laid it on her desktop and with the back of her hand tried to smooth its wrinkles. She brought it to Mr. Morey. The signed permission slip. It had been buried there for three days, forgotten. "Go give it to Mrs. Schaefer," he said, shaking his head. Hydea skipped out of the room, officially a member of Mrs. Keefe's winter reading group. She couldn't wait to tell Grandma.

M̲r. Hay, much better at addressing adults than Hydea, was experiencing a communication problem of his own. A few weeks earlier, he had sent home notices to every parent, asking their attendance at a half-hour meeting to discuss the school budget as well as the terms of the teacher-parent-student compact that was at the heart of Brookside's shared plan for student achievement. One parent had showed.

As the head of a Title I school, Mr. Hay was required by the federal NCLB law to consult parents on all key aspects of school management. Empowering parents to assume an active role in decisions about their children's education was one of the centerpieces of the legislation. Throughout his eight years at Brookside, he said, parental input had been almost nil. He would schedule a community meeting and one or two parents would show. At his most successful gathering, attendance reached three. Mr. Hay was at a loss at what to do. He had tried scheduling the meetings in the morning, in the afternoon, in the evening. Every Hispanic household received a flyer written in Spanish. Nothing had worked. He fantasized about attracting Mrs. Schaefer's parent workshop crowd of 125. A turnout of just 25 would have had him turning cartwheels. All those stories in the media about activist parents marching the streets, shaking up their neighborhood schools, he said. He hadn't seen anything like that at Brookside. "You'd think parents would want some say in how we spend our $140,000 in Title I money this year," he said. He had toyed with piggybacking the next meeting on the night of Mrs. Schaefer's second reading workshop for parents. "I could schedule it half an hour before her session. Maybe people would come if they were already planning to be at the school anyway," he mused.

Mr. Hay wasn't the only one at Brookside troubled by a lack of parent participation. Across the hallway, Audra Good, the PTO president, sat in her own office at a long cafeteria table covered with boxes and papers and wrestled with why Marbella's parents and Hydea's grandmother, and minority parents and guardians in general, had shown little interest in her organization. After all, she said, the PTO's entire purpose was to raise money for Brookside's students and otherwise support the school. Over the course of the 2010–11 academic year, she said, the PTO would sponsor a multicultural, pot luck family night dinner, host a series of schoolwide educational assemblies, and raise enough money through a silent auction and fund-raising events to bankroll class field trips to, among other places, New York's American Museum of Natural History and Carnegie Hall. Who wouldn't want that? Annual membership dues, she said, were more than reasonable: $5 for families that joined at the start of the school year, $7 thereafter, with free memberships available for those who couldn't afford the fee.

So far this year, Mrs. Good said, 110 families had joined. But of those, only about 40 were active, and the vast majority, like Mrs. Good, were middle class and white. The membership was "not as diverse as the school, I have to admit," she said. Mrs. Good continued. "There are some Hispanic parents who are involved," she said, "a few African Americans. But they're more of a middle-class background."

Marbella's family was middle class. So was Hydea's. Still, neither had joined the PTO. For Hydea's grandmother, it was a matter of limited time and interest. But Marbella's mother had a different concern. Right or wrong, she felt the PTO was somewhat exclusionary, that she was made to feel she didn't belong. Seated in her neat, comfortable living room, she said with some resentment, "I feel that those parents are just all about themselves. You know, they've been members so long, I just feel like if you try to get in, they're going to look at you like, 'Who are you and why are you coming here?'"

It was a common impression, Mrs. Good admitted, seated in her office, that was hard to overcome. Only last year, she said, the organization's executive board had called a special meeting, inviting the parents of Brookside's Hispanic students to help figure a way to bridge the PTO's membership gap. Just five Hispanic parents had attended. To date, she said, the group had implemented no initiatives to attract black members. "With the Hispanic families," Mrs. Good said, "there's a language barrier to break. With the African American families, I don't know what that barrier is."

Among the Brookside students, no such barriers existed. On the playground and in the cafeteria, the two places they had free choice, blacks, Hispanics, and white; middle class and poor; girls and boys; talkative children and quiet all mixed together. Their cliques were determined differently. At one picnic-style table in the lunchroom sat the louder, more demonstrative children— Marbella, Aajah, and Hydea (never loud or demonstrative, but she clung to her friends) along with Carlos and Chandler and two others—four blacks, one Hispanic, one mixed race, one white. At another were most of the better students—among them, Jacky, Dennis (he had the ability if not the desire to be a good student), Kyle, and Josh—one Hispanic, three whites. Scattered between them were a mishmash of unaffiliated classmates. For the most part, with the exception of Marbella and Fernando, they all got along. "Elementary school is such an intimate experience," Mr. Morey said, watching his students carouse on the playground during recess one afternoon. "They're together all day, in the same classroom, with the same teacher who looks after them all. It's like a big family. They get to know each other so well. They don't understand how different it's going to be next year, in middle school, when they move from class to class and they don't see each other as much and new kids coming from other elementary schools enter the scene. They're a little older, a little more mature, maybe, and they develop new interests. That's when friendships start to change."

Mr. Morey knew if he had told any of that to Marbella, Hydea, and Aajah, they wouldn't have believed him. Just recently, Aajah had gotten a phone with a conferencing feature, and the girls now spent their afternoons gossiping away. Aajah and Hydea teased Marbella that she liked Carlos. Marbella protested mightily. One day Aajah mentioned her coming birthday, in February. "My mom says I can invite you," she said. "She says she'll take us to City Island"—a tiny residential island in the Bronx, New York—"where they have all these great seafood places. Wanna go?"

The girls grew giddy with excitement. Once, in fourth grade, Hydea and Aajah had met for a playdate at a neighborhood park. That was the sum of their socializing. The three started to make plans—what they'd wear, the food they'd order, whether Aajah's mom would secretly arrange for a birthday cake. The anticipation drew them even closer; now it was like they had their own special club. The phone calls between them increased. Sometimes Hydea thought it would be fun if the three of them arranged a playdate before the party. But she never brought it up, and the others didn't, either. Maybe seeing each other in school every day was enough, Hydea decided. Anyway, she couldn't very well invite the girls to her apartment. Hydea shared a bedroom with her older sister, Billi, and she knew Billi would do something that would totally embarrass her. Maybe, she thought, Marbella and Aajah worried that their older siblings would do the same.

At school, the three play-acted more and more in Hydea's fantasy world of Rabia. No one else had access. Another girl wanted in, but they wouldn't share the secret password. Mr. Morey knew about it, but didn't mind, as long as it remained playful and didn't interfere with their classwork. He knew from experience how fragile a child's focus could be. Across the hallway in Mrs. Bohrer's room, a boy named Edwin had fallen tragically, unrequitedly in love with his classmate Carol, who sat directly opposite him, and his work and attitude had instantly tumbled. A potential benefit, Mr. Morey thought, was that Hydea's friendship with the girls might boost her self-confidence. At home, Hydea's grandmother was cheered that she was so happy.

That afternoon, Aajah phoned Hydea at home. "Promise me something," she said. "When we go in the car to City Island, you can't talk about Justin Bieber." One whisper of his name, she reminded her, and Marbella would never shut up about him. Aajah was already sick of the singer. On that October day, Bieber was the only issue that stood between the three girls.

Chapter 4

M r. Morey had reason to worry about his class, especially in
math. Except for Josh, Kyle, and Jacky, no one was faring
particularly well. One morning he handed the students a sheet of
fifteen pre-algebra problems to solve. He wasn't sure how many
understood the theory involved. The day before, in the course of
teaching a lesson on the subject, he had written two number val-
ues, an equation and two questions on the whiteboard.

$x = 10, y = 5$

$x + y = 15$

What is the value of x? What is the value of y?

"Hydea," he had asked. "What's another word for *equal*?"

"I don't know," she had said, ducking her head.

"Marbella?"

"Total?"

To both girls' relief, Kyle had raised his hand. "The same," he had answered.

Well, at least someone knew, Mr. Morey had thought. Now, how to explain the concept in a way the rest would understand? He had turned to the whiteboard and drawn a seesaw balanced on a fulcrum. On one end of the seesaw he had written 5 + 6. At the opposite end he wrote 11. "Hydea," he asked, "If you want to balance a seesaw and you put five plus six on one side and eleven on the other, what does that mean?"

"They're equal," she had said, with confidence now.

"How do you know?"

"Because five plus six is eleven, so they're the same," she had answered.

Mr. Morey had erased the five and replaced it with an x. "What does x equal?" he had asked.

Hydea had hesitated, staring at the board. "Five?"

"Perfect," Mr. Morey had said. "Boys and girls, does everybody get that? Does everyone see what Hydea did?" All had nodded in agreement. Mr. Morey hadn't been convinced. From past experience, he knew at least three or four would have been too embarrassed to admit they didn't understand. That was the reason for today's drill. He'd spot those having trouble and work with each at their desk, one-on-one. The first five problems, solving for x and y, read:

$$x + 9 = 26$$
$$42 + y = 57$$
$$x - 32 = 49$$

$$45 + y = 98$$
$$x + 23 = 92$$

Progress for most was painfully slow. Dennis, clearly uninterested in the assignment, stared into space. Mr. Morey barked at him. Grudgingly, he went to work. Carlos crossed the room for a drink of water. Josh and Kyle breezed through the questions, Jacky answered them methodically, but accurately. Marbella and Hydea, like half a dozen of their classmates, bit their lower lip, counted on their fingers, and made liberal use of their pencil erasers. Mr. Morey was disturbed by the number of finger counters. It meant that a quarter of their way through fifth grade, his students still had trouble adding and subtracting. Few were on firm ground with their multiplication tables past three. How would they ever master long division, let alone pre-algebra or working with fractions? he wondered. It was apparent they had spent little if any time—as he had at their age—practicing with their parents with flash cards at home. He wondered what more he could do. His eyes fell on Chris. What he witnessed was riveting. The ten-year-old worked for several minutes, then laid his head on his desk. Over the next five minutes he proceeded to raise his head, stretch his lips wide with his index fingers, twist his lower lip with his right hand, stare at Chandler seated opposite him, return his attention to the math sheet and count to forty-three on both hands to solve question four, count out the answer to another question, clench his teeth and erase what he had just written, sneeze, stick his right index finger in his right ear, refigure the question that had stumped him, stare into space, stare at the wall clock, catch Chandler's gaze and make a face, do more computation with his fingers, eye Aajah seated nearby him, place his index fingers in his mouth, play with a miniature action figure he pulled from his desk, and finally place his chin on his desk.

Mr. Morey chose not to single out Chris. Instead, he collected the papers and sat on a worktable beneath the whiteboard, at the front of the room. "Boys and girls," he said. "I was watching you. A lot of you had trouble staying focused for two minutes. On the CMT, you're going to have to stay focused for forty-five minutes. I can teach you the formulas. I can teach you the strategies. But what's the one thing I can't do for you?"

"Make us concentrate." Chandler said.

"You need to develop stamina, just like an athlete," Mr. Morey urged them. "The only way to do that is practice, practice, practice." He clapped his hands like a coach. From the children's reactions, they didn't appear ready to charge out and win one for Brookside, and Mr. Morey. He decided to save his pep talk on the importance of knowing their math facts for another day.

M r. Morey wasn't the only staff member disappointed with his students and their parents. Mrs. Keefe had just received a call from the mother of one of her fifth graders.

"How dare you criticize my child," the mother had snapped. Earlier that day Mrs. Keefe had given the boy a poor grade and had challenged him to work harder, explaining he was too bright to waste his intelligence by underachieving. She told the mother what she'd said, adding that her son had a tendency to start projects— start them well—but never complete them.

"That's the kind of student I was," the mother had responded.

"Then you should understand what I'm doing, that I'm trying to get the best out of your child."

"No," the mother had corrected her. "I was the kind of student who did the work on subjects that I liked, and didn't on the ones I didn't like. That's what I want for my son. If he doesn't want to learn something, I don't want you demanding that he does."

While the woman talked, Mrs. Keefe heard a daytime soap opera playing in the background.

One Friday Mr. Hay stood in the main office, bagging weekend care packages for Brookside's twenty-four neediest students. It ensured that they'd have food till school, and its free breakfast and lunch programs for the poor, resumed on Monday. One child was in Mr. Morey's class. Assembling the packages was among the most gratifying moments of Mr. Hay's week. He knew what that food meant to the students and their families. He had petitioned the Connecticut Food Bank, a New Haven charity, to be the provider. That day, each care package contained two single-serving boxes of cold cereal, two juice drinks, two containers of 2 percent milk, franks and beans, tuna in a pouch, two single-serving packages of brown rice, two fruit bars, and applesauce.

He was halfway through when he was interrupted. A school volunteer reported trouble in Mr. Morey's room. Mr. Morey was absent that day, the student teacher who was substituting for him had lost control of the room and Marbella had been hurt. Fernando had knocked the wind out of her. (To save money, rather than hire a substitute teacher, the school sometimes turned to its student teachers to fill in.)

The volunteer described a scene of mayhem. The student teacher had attempted to direct a vocabulary lesson, but few students had paid attention. Around the room, children were chattering. The student teacher had raised her voice, trying to enforce quiet. The children, led by Carlos and Chandler, had grown louder and more disruptive. Several talked back, refusing to work. The student teacher, overwhelmed, had turned to the clock, wishing she could advance it forward to 11:30. That was the time Officer Christopher Holmes, a Norwalk police officer and the department's DARE (Drug Abuse Resistance Education) representative, was scheduled to arrive. Each Friday, he instructed the class on the dangers of substance abuse. The student teacher had assumed the students would calm down with a policeman in the room. But when Officer Holmes stepped through the door, the situation immediately had turned worse. The policeman was popular with the students, and with Mr. Morey not around to enforce discipline, half the children had leaped from their seats and raced to embrace him. Marbella and Fernando had reached Officer Holmes at the same time. Fernando, unschooled in chivalry and not fond of Marbella anyway (earlier, the student teacher had caught him making faces and mouthing inappropriate words at Marbella), had elbowed her in the stomach, knocking the wind from her and sending her to the ground. Fernando had then made his way, triumphant, to the officer's side.

It had taken a few seconds for those in the room to realize what had occurred. Chaos had then ensued. While Officer Holmes knelt down and attended to Marbella, the rest of the students had gone unsupervised. Fernando had run to his desk, buried his head in his hands and had started crying. "I made a bad decision," he had repeated again and again. At some point during the havoc, an unidentified student had grabbed an indelible, red-ink marker and scrawled an uneven line down the lower left corner of Mr. Morey's $2,000 SMART Board, defacing it.

Mr. Hay hurried to Mr. Morey's room. The students turned deathly quiet as he escorted Fernando out the door. By then Marbella had regained her breath, if not her composure. She left the room, sniffling, to see the school nurse. (She was unhurt.) The class remained subdued the rest of the day.

Fernando spent part of the afternoon in Mr. Hay's office, twiddling his thumbs, seated quietly in a high-back chair, waiting for his mother to arrive to take him home. It wasn't the first time he'd been in trouble for striking a girl. Not long before, he had pinched and pushed a fourth grader on the school bus. Much to the surprise of those who had witnessed the episode, Mr. Hay did not suspend Fernando. "If I send him home for three days, he'll just sit there watching TV, having a good time," he reasoned. He was probably right. Fernando's father worked long hours as a day laborer, and he left discipline to his wife. His wife, who spoke little English, confessed to Mr. Hay through the school's bilingual social worker that she no longer could control her son.

So much had happened since the children had recited the Pledge of Allegiance that morning. They had all but forgotten that following the pledge, they had sung "Happy Birthday" to one of their classmates. Fernando had turned eleven that day.

Mr. Morey had stewed all weekend about his class. He'd learned about Fernando, Marbella, the class's meltdown, and his defaced SMART Board Friday afternoon. Now, sitting at his desk Monday an hour before his first students arrived, he had to decide what to do. This wasn't the first time trouble had erupted in his room. Once before, the class had overrun a substitute. On another occasion, they had turned the room into a noisy playground the instant he had stepped into the hallway to confer with Mrs. Bohrer. Two issues faced him. Both, Mr. Morey knew, threatened his control of the room. The smaller one concerned Fernando. He had been the spark on Friday, but he hadn't lit the fuse. Fernando was a follower—more of an irritant, Mr. Morey thought—one who gained attention by acting out or making silly remarks but who had few allies in class, let alone real friends. Had others not been loud and disruptive, had others obeyed the student teacher, he was certain Fernando would have remained in his seat. The larger issue was the two disrupters—Carlos and Chandler. Both were popular and, as their fourth-grade teacher could attest, able to influence how others behaved. Somehow, Mr. Morey knew, he was going to have to win one of them over. But which one? And how?

Mr. Morey considered Carlos. Crew-cut Carlos was not only a good athlete but charming and funny and full of bravado, with a mischievous smile that lit up a room. Yet few of his classmates sensed how needy he was. Several years earlier his parents had divorced, and it had affected him deeply. "We used to have a lot of heart-to-hearts," Miss Sutton, his third-grade teacher, said. Though Carlos didn't tell anyone, from time to time throughout fifth grade, he still stopped by her room to talk. Mr. Morey understood Carlos's situation better than most. Three years earlier, he had taught his older sister. Like Miss Sutton, he saw through Carlos's cocky facade. In fact, to boost his confidence, he had introduced the boy to a troubled third grader. "I want you to be his friend, be like a mentor," Mr. Morey had said, after consulting with the younger boy's teacher. Carlos had leaped at the opportunity. Periodically, during independent reading, Mr. Morey would send him down the hall to the third grader's room, to sit next to him in class. Throughout the early part of the school year, Carlos had visited with the boy once a week, sometimes more. Mr. Morey was pleased. "I'm hoping it will help Carlos mature," he said. He knew what others didn't— that Carlos wasn't a leader.

That left Chandler. He was a tall, husky African American with an easy smile and wavy black hair. He was good at all sports, especially football, and possessed a world of charisma and a wonderful smile. Girls liked him. Boys did, too. He was a decent student, Mr. Morey thought, with the potential to do much better if he only tried. Had Mr. Morey asked, Chandler would have admitted he was more interested in being the funny man, the class clown. That had been his reputation throughout much of his Brookside career. He and Carlos had been classmates since second grade. Carlos had come to his last birthday party. They had been teammates in a recreational Biddy Basketball league. Together, they had dictated the character of their classrooms. It was a mystery to the teachers why Mr. Hay hadn't split them up. Mr. Morey's eyes followed Chandler as he shuffled into the room and settled in his seat. Chandler caught his look. He knew he was in trouble for Friday's class meltdown. Everyone knew they were in trouble.

Mr. Morey had wanted to address the matter right away; he wasn't the type to let things fester. But the students got a temporary reprieve. Mr. Hay had scheduled a visit from High Touch High Tech, an educational firm that sends whimsical, white-smocked science instructors to schools to conduct fun, hands-on demonstrations of the laws of science. For an hour, Mr. Morey's class learned about the mysteries of sound.

The moment the instructor rolled his portable lab out the door, Mr. Morey called the students to the rug at the front of the room. He sat on a worktable, his legs stretched out in front of him. The students braced for a thunder of words. They never came. Instead, Mr. Morey spoke quietly, as if he were exhausted. "Our class is absolutely horrible when I'm not here," he began. "We've got students assaulting other students, students defacing school property, students acting in class like it's recess. I understand it's not everybody, but the ones who weren't misbehaving weren't stopping the ones that were. The worst part is, you can't be trusted. That's just sad." His eyes passed over every student in the room. No one uttered a sound.

He turned to Fernando. He wanted to drive home a message. Fernando is Mexican, and Mr. Morey knew how important the concept of manhood is to his culture. "If you don't know how to treat women," he told him, "then you're not a man. A man does not hit women. Neither does a boy."

He addressed the rest of the class. "This is my tenth year of teaching," he said. "For nine years, my classes all did pretty much the same thing. They all acted up on the sub." He raised his right index finger. "One time. That's the key. One time. And then they learned. This is the third time for this class. You're not learning. I guess that's my fault." He shook his head and pointed to the inked line on the bottom corner of the SMART Board. "I've had this board for six years. Never in six years has someone defaced it. This is the only fifth-grade class with a SMART Board. I use it to teach you. At recess you play games on it. Why anyone would do such a thing, I don't even know." No one confessed, no one made a sound. Mr. Morey sighed. He told them he was taking away their snack time and recess for a month, and that their planned class Christmas party was very much up in the air. "I'm pretty much out of words. Anybody have anything to say?" he asked. Silence. "Chandler, do you have anything to say?" The boy shook his head no. "Do you know why I'm calling on you?" Another shake no. "I'm looking for leaders," Mr. Morey said. "I'm looking for leaders who will step up and solve the problem. Someone who will step up and stop stuff. That's the difference between this class and my other classes. They had leaders. Right now, you don't." He sent them back to their seats.

A tense day passed. Every student sought invisibility. Anything to avoid Mr. Morey's radar. The following afternoon, while the rest of the class was doing their independent reading, Mr. Morey asked Chandler to follow him into the hallway. Chandler's shoulders slumped; he figured he was in trouble yet again. It seemed he and Mr. Morey had been butting heads for weeks. Several times, the teacher had phoned his parents.

"Chandler," Mr. Morey said, "kids in the classroom look up to you, right?"

"Yeah," he said, unsure of what Mr. Morey was getting at.

"So you're a leader, right?"

"I guess so."

"Well, you're not acting like a leader," Mr. Morey said. "If you goof around, what's everyone going to do?"

"They're probably going to play around."

"Don't you see, Chandler, they listen to you because they respect you. So start acting like a leader. Start doing the right things. You've got to step up. If you get your stuff together, it's going to have a big effect on the rest of the class. I need your help."

Chandler didn't know what to say. "Okay," he said, noncommittally.

"All right, you can go back in the room," Mr. Morey said. Whether his message had gotten through, he couldn't say.

Mrs. Schaefer was growing increasingly frustrated with the three fifth-grade teachers. Each week she met with them to review their students' progress and map out aspects of the reading comprehension and writing curriculum they should cover next. The problem was, there was little continuity in the styles they taught. According to the curriculum plan, all were supposed to adhere to the Reading and Writing Project workshop model. But Mrs. Keefe didn't really see the value to it, and taught her own way, Mrs. Bohrer was more comfortable as a traditional teacher than as a collaborator or coach, and Mr. Morey preferred to cherry-pick the material he taught, choosing material from both the workshop workbook and from an old basal anthology he kept in his room. During independent reading, the teachers seldom circulated the room as the workshop program called for, conferencing with students on issues of plot, character, theme, and the like. Nor, except on rare occasions, did they ask students to discuss their reading among themselves. Mrs. Keefe and Mrs. Bohrer generally were fastidious about collecting and recording data; Mr. Morey tended to be lackadaisical. At one meeting, looking ahead to the CMT, Mrs. Schaefer asked the three to assign their students a particular exercise in expository writing. She explained precisely the criteria by which they were to grade them. "A two is passing," she said. "A two means they captured the main point of the article, gave two examples from the text that support the main point, gave two details, also from the text, that support each example, and wrote a coherent conclusion. A one means they missed one or more key elements, but got the gist of it. A zero means they were completely lost." The next week, when they met to review the students' papers, Mrs. Schaefer quickly realized that what one teacher had graded a two, another had judged to be a one. And sometimes vice versa. How was she, or they, to determine the students' true needs? It reiterated her belief that the fifth-grade teachers were the least disciplined group in the school. In earlier years, she had complained to Mr. Hay about them, but he'd had bigger issues on his plate and had been lukewarm about getting involved. Without his backing, Mrs. Schaefer was in a tricky spot. She was the literacy expert, not an administrator. She lacked the power to unilaterally direct the faculty what to teach or how. All she could do was suggest. It was a shame, Mrs. Schaefer thought. Often, she wondered how much the students would achieve if the three teachers cooperated better and fully committed themselves to the workshop model. She returned to her office, vaguely depressed as she was after almost every fifth-grade meeting, thinking, We'll never get the chance to find out.

Mrs. Schaefer shut the door and pulled her chair to her desk—the only adult furniture in the office. She had put a great deal of thought into the room's furnishings and layout. She had designed it to be part children's library, part cocoon. Tiny, inviting, it was the most intimate room in the school. Books hugged every wall, covered nearly every surface. They filled bins, lined shelves. There were books big and small, nonfiction, and fiction in a variety of genres, with colorful, *Pick me!* covers loud as bursts of fireworks. Most were targeted to emerging readers—kindergarten and first- and second-grade students. Mrs. Schaefer considered them her true constituency. To her, there was nothing more vital than taking a struggling child—one lacking confidence, who knew already at age six or seven that he was lagging behind his classmates—and giving him the tools and strategies to help him catch up, to succeed. Whatever her failings addressing a roomful of adults, the children with whom she worked in the privacy of her office, one-on-one, saw her as their advocate, as the educator, more than any, who could teach them to read. She had a way of taking on their knottiest problems—ones their classroom teachers couldn't solve—and making things clear. "My first-grade teacher sent me to Mrs. Schaefer," Kevin, now in Mrs. Bohrer's class, recalled. Kevin was a terrific artist, skilled at portraiture and sketching his favorite action figures, but a fumbling reader. By the end of first grade, he was already frustrated, almost a year behind, performing at Level 4 when grade level was 16. Each day for half an hour, he and Mrs. Schaefer had sat side by side at a children's desk, seated in children's chairs, facing away from the hallway so they wouldn't be disturbed by passing students as he read aloud. "I was having trouble when there would be a new word," Kevin remembered. "I would try to sound it out but I never got the word. Like, the first time I heard *spectacular* I tried to pronounce it, but I kept on getting it wrong. Mrs. Schaefer told me to find smaller parts in it, to cut it into pieces. And then I pronounced it and I was happy."

This year, though, fewer and fewer students had come walking through her door. In accordance with the current Title I mandate, she had spent the bulk of her time in the lower-grade classrooms mentoring teachers on the finer points of Reading and Writing Project workshop instruction. During these sessions, she would observe a classroom teacher as she conducted a mini lesson or worked with a group of three or four students. Later, she and the teacher would critique the teacher's performance. Indirectly, Mrs. Schaefer knew, she was impacting far more children through improved classroom tutelage than she ever could by working with students individually. Still, the feeling wasn't quite the same. She missed that *ah ha!* moment, when a child with whom she had been working for weeks finally got it, when the lesson she'd been teaching kicked in.

One morning a few weeks before Thanksgiving, she visited Mrs. Walker's second-grade classroom. Mrs. Walker was one of her favorites. Dark haired, bubbly, a mentor to many of her younger colleagues, Mrs. Walker had been teaching for thirty-five years, the last twenty-two at Brookside. Like so many college-educated women of her generation, she had known since childhood what her profession would be. "When I was twelve, I ran my own school in the house where I grew up on the Jersey shore," Mrs. Walker recalled, seated at her classroom desk one morning an hour before her first students arrived. "I had the neighbors coming over for school. I had an easel, a lot of paper and pencils and lots of books.

I taught a lot of math and a lot of reading. It probably mirrored what I learned in school that day." Mrs. Walker was one of the first Brookside teachers to buy into the workshop program. For three summers, she attended the same intensive training sessions at Columbia that Mrs. Schaefer had. The coursework had affirmed every shortcoming of basal readers that over time she, like Mrs. Schaefer, had come to believe. For years she had shopped after school at Goodwill stores and through children's book clubs, seeking alternative titles that might appeal to both her advanced and reluctant readers. "I've bought thousands of books," she said, pointing to the stuffed bins that filled her shelves. Now, since Mr. Hay had adopted the workshop system, the school did the bulk of the buying.

Several of the children turned their heads when Mrs. Schaefer entered Mrs. Walker's room. Just one stood up from his seat and approached her—Matthew, a tow-haired, seven-year-old she had spent considerable time with the previous year. Mrs. Schaefer could tell from Matthew's expression that he was both hopeful and sad. More than once he had stopped her in the hallway. "Can I read with you?" he would ask.

Mrs. Schaefer never knew what to say. Since the beginning of the school year, she had seen Matthew just once or twice. Title I's new mandate that she spend the bulk of her time training teachers in reading and writing instruction had limited her availability to individual students. Come January, with CMT prep, her ability to see second graders such as Matthew would disappear almost entirely. Second graders did not take the CMT. Mrs. Schaefer knew there was no way she could explain this to him. "Matthew," she had told him, gently, "I'd love to read with you, and when I do have a moment, I promise I will grab you."

Saying no to Matthew—turning down a child in need—cut against everything Mrs. Schaefer stood for. Like Mrs. Walker, Mrs. Schaefer believed she had been born to teach. "I *always* knew. *Always*. Growing up, I just never had any other desires," she said, seated in a child's chair, legs tucked beneath a child's table, in her office. More specifically, she had wanted to teach elementary school. Maybe it was because of her own upbringing, she thought. Growing up, first in the Bronx and later in suburban Irvington, New York, she had had to tackle school pretty much by herself. Her parents, neither of whom had attended college, had not been home much; they had worked long hours at the several area Jewish delis they owned. Their absence had forced Mrs. Schaefer to be independent, and her internal drive had propelled her through public school and then college. She considered herself fortunate; other latchkey children at her schools had struggled. Those were the ones, she decided, that she could one day help. Mrs. Schaefer began her career preparations early. For her eighth birthday, she asked her parents for a slate blackboard "just like the ones in school." Thereafter, she played teacher, she said, with her friends, dolls, and older sister (who, briefly, went on to teach at an elementary school as well).

In 1969, after earning her education degree at the University of Bridgeport, Mrs. Schaefer began teaching third grade in Stamford. (Later, she returned to her alma mater and completed her master's degree.) Her first year, she taught from a basal reader, a standard language arts anthology employed by all the third-grade teachers.

Frustrated by the number of students either unable to grasp the material, or bored to tears by it, she asked her principal the following year if she could try a fresh strategy of her own. "I told him I just didn't think that kids could learn to read all from the same book," she said. It was an opinion, really. Back then, there was no test to definitively assess a child's reading level. As it happened, the principal shared her concern. He gave her permission to experiment. She checked out armfuls of children's books from the school and town libraries, some easier to read, some more challenging, and matched them to the individual needs of her students. She tried grouping her students in unusual ways, teaming higher-level readers with lower-level ones, hoping the children would learn from one another. She trotted out half a dozen different strategies. Not all her ideas worked. "It was trial by error," she said.

Mrs. Schaefer convened a weekly, after-school brainstorming session with several like-minded colleagues. She floated more ideas. Why not supplant the stories in the anthology with ones of her own? Why not have students create their own stories? "I had kids making their own books," she said. "My thinking was, if they can think, they can write, and if they write, they can read." One day at the library, she checked out a variety of children's books on the solar system, all written at different reading levels. The next afternoon, during science period, she distributed them to her students according to their reading ability. She found, after the students had finished reading, that she was able to teach a lesson on the planets they could all understand and, furthermore, discuss. It was a revelation. Her next five teaching years were a joy. Then she placed her career on hold, following the birth of the first of her three children. "My husband [then an Arnold Bread distributor] and I had always agreed I'd leave teaching to raise our kids," she said. Her hiatus lasted twelve years.

It was no secret in her household that Mrs. Schaefer missed teaching. For a while, she taught secular classes part-time in a Jewish elementary/middle school. It only whetted her desire to resume her career. In 1988, when her youngest was twelve, she learned of an opening for a third-grade teacher at Brookside. She jumped at it. The only downside was the basal reader the school employed. She'd have to begin her campaign for differentiation all over again, she thought. Then she met Holly Balsinger.

Mrs. Balsinger, Brookside's Reading Recovery teacher, had been hired in 1995, when the district had money to invest in experimental programs. Petite, blond, inquisitive, she was not a classroom instructor. A trained literacy specialist, her job was to take the lowest-achieving first-grade readers—those who had not mastered the complex skills required to read and write—and work with them one-on-one, daily, for half an hour, for a period of twelve to twenty weeks, until, it was hoped, the students reached grade level, ready to return full-time to their classroom, in a position to achieve. Reading Recovery targeted first graders because it was the most efficient place to catch and retrain deficient readers. Developed by New Zealand educator Marie Clay and introduced in 1984 to the United States, it was more a teaching philosophy than a program. Research showed it had a success rate of approximately 75 percent.

The idea behind Reading Recovery was deceptively simple: Focus not on a child's reading weaknesses but on implementing the strategies that enable good readers to succeed. "If you think about what you are doing when you're reading," Mrs. Balsinger explained, one afternoon at her home, "you're integrating meaning—what's happening in the text—with syntax or structure—what's going to sound right, and with visual information—what's going to look right on the page. A proficient reader integrates those three reading cues automatically. If a good reader is reading and something doesn't make sense, that child will go back and reread, looking for certain cues. But a struggling child doesn't know to do that, doesn't know that that's going to help." She gave an example. "Say a child is reading and comes across a tricky or difficult word, like *nest*. And there is a picture in the book that shows a bird making a nest. A teacher can give that child a hint: 'You know, it's something that a bird makes in a tree.' And the child will say, 'Nest.' But that does not make him accountable. Because if the teacher weren't there to give him the clue, how would he come up with it himself? So instead, the teacher might say, 'Look at the picture. What do you think it could be? Get your mouth ready to say the first sound.' You can teach children prompts they can replicate themselves, so when they get stuck, when they're reading without you, they can say, 'Oh, wait a minute. I can look at the picture and I can think, what's going to make sense, what's going to sound right from the letters, and I can say the word.'"

Mrs. Schaefer was fascinated with Reading Recovery. She read everything she could on Marie Clay and her philosophy. It was the first time she had seen scientific evidence of how children learned to read. She broached one of her ideas to Mrs. Balsinger. What if we third-grade teachers scheduled an extra, afternoon reading period, she asked. One teacher would take all of the grade's advanced readers. Another would take the average achievers. Mrs. Schaefer proposed to teach the ones who were struggling. Mrs. Balsinger and the other teachers agreed to try it.

It proved a turning point in Mrs. Schaefer's career. Mrs. Balsinger and a special education teacher came to her room to help. They divided the children into three groups. Together they taught a lesson, with Mrs. Balsinger mentoring her colleagues on Reading Recovery teaching techniques. Weeks passed. Mrs. Schaefer was struck by the degree they were able to raise the children's ability. "I still remember a book I used with the kids in my little group, *The Beast in Ms. Rooney's Room*," she recalled. "It was a paperback that we read and talked about. I still remember those kids being so excited and saying, 'This is the first book I ever read by myself and finished.' I made them all a certificate saying, 'I finished this book.'" Mrs. Schaefer began spending more time with Mrs. Balsinger, intent on picking her brain.

In 1998, when the Board of Education decided to create a second Reading Recovery position for Brookside, Mrs. Schaefer was quick to apply. Following an intensive, year-plus training program, she and Mrs. Balsinger worked as a team. But their period together lasted just five years. In 2003, shortly before Mr. Hay arrived, the school board initiated what would become an era of budget cuts, and eliminated Reading Recovery throughout the district. Mrs. Schaefer wasn't entirely surprised. Over the course of a school year, she and Mrs. Balsinger had worked with a maximum of thirty-two students—a poor return on a pair of specialists commanding relatively high salaries, to the board members' eyes. Mrs. Balsinger transferred to another Norwalk elementary school, while Mrs. Schaefer remained at Brookside. Both were reassigned to their current positions as literacy coaches. Ironically, Mr. Hay had championed Reading Recovery at his last Massachusetts school; it was one of the reasons for his interest in Brookside.

Mrs. Schaefer had made her peace, as best she could, with the limits CMT prep had placed on her job. After all, what option did she have? Still, she regretted not being able to continue her work with Matthew. Through her tutelage, by the end of first grade he had made halting progress, and now, without the extra support she had provided him, much of it had washed away.

She remembered the first time Matthew had appeared on her radar, the previous February. Mrs. Gilroy, his highly regarded first-grade teacher, had come to her seeking advice. Matthew had begun the school year at grade level, but almost immediately his progress had stalled. By midwinter he was among the lowest achievers in her class. Among his weaknesses, she had said, was an inability to gather his thoughts and put them in writing. He knew the alphabet and could form letters, but he struggled when it came to combining them into words, phrases, sentences. At the heart of his difficulty was his inability to recognize what were known as sight words—common words that appear regularly in reading. He'd get stuck on them and be unable to read any further. "He'd just shut down, stop trying, stop reading," Mrs. Gilroy had said. She couldn't understand why. Matthew was of average intelligence. Some of the words that perplexed him were right in front of him, posted on the classroom walls. As Mrs. Gilroy did for all her students, she had helped him create his own personal folder of sight words. The two called it his "word wall." Whenever Matthew had come to her with a sight word he had difficulty spelling, such as *would* or *could*, Mrs. Gilroy had added it to his wall. But little of her strategy had worked. Matthew was hypersensitive, often moody, and Mrs. Gilroy had confessed that some days she'd had trouble reaching him. With twenty-one students, she had only so much time to give. He needed someone at home, she had said, to sit with him and help him put pencil to paper.

From what Mrs. Schaefer knew of Matthew's family, she feared that wouldn't be easy. At home, he lived in the shadow of his thirteen-year-old brother, Daniel, a brilliant student (when he put his mind to it), with whom he shared a prickly relationship. Daniel sometimes agreed to help Matthew with his homework but charged his parents $5 an hour to do so (adding, as only an older brother would, "I don't normally charge for playing with him, but I probably should"). Matthew's parents read with him around 8:30, shortly before his bedtime, but seldom had time to offer additional help. Both worked unusually long hours; his mother as a veterinarian at two pet clinics who periodically served on the overnight shift, his father as the office manager at one of the clinics. His mother also ran a small horse stable. Most days, neither was home to see Matthew off to school or to sit with him at dinner. Matthew was forced to turn to the family's nanny, a middle-aged, high school–educated woman whose primary function was to care for his three-year-old brother, for homework assistance.

A few days after discussing Matthew with Mrs. Gilroy, Mrs. Schaefer had pulled the six-year-old from class to assess his reading level and identify his strengths and weaknesses. Mrs. Gilroy had been right; he scored at Level 6 when he should have been at

Level 16 or 18. His fluency was poor, his reading robotic and halt-ing, and he was waylaid by the simplest sight words. After half a year of first grade, he had barely progressed.

Mrs. Schaefer scheduled the first of several meetings she would have with his parents. Knowing they had transferred Matthew's homework responsibilities primarily to the nanny, she had asked that they bring her along. The four met in Mrs. Schaefer's office, where they all sat around a child-size conference table in child-size chairs. Mrs. Schaefer had explained Matthew's major weaknesses and then had instructed them on the basics of how to teach read-ing. She had given them the following list of sight words: *here, are, they, went, car, come, shouted, this, with, all, was.* "I told them they could play a game with him," she said. "Every time Matthew reads one of those words correctly and says it automatically, he gets a check. And when he gets five checks on a word, that means he re-ally knows it, and you can write it into a memory book you create for him, and he can move on to other high-frequency words." She had then described Mrs. Balsinger's strategy for getting any child, struggling or bright, to suss out words on their own.

She had given them other tips, as well: Teach him, as Mrs. Gilroy had been doing, that when he got stuck on a word, he should look at the accompanying picture and try to match the word to it. Or he could reread the sentence and try to understand the word in context. Or he could break the word down into letters or syllables, making it easier to sound out. "The idea," Mrs. Schaefer had said, "is, so when he's reading without you, he can say, 'Oh wait a min-ute. I can look at the picture, and I can think what's going to make sense, and I can say the word.'"

Matthew's parents had never heard those techniques before.

They had promised to try them with Matthew at home, as time allowed. Mrs. Schaefer had offered some out-of-classroom advice. "I told them how needy Matthew was, how he was always seeking special attention in class. 'If you could just set up a special time for him,' I told them. I said to the dad, 'If you could take just Matthew out for ice cream without his brothers, so he gets one-on-one time with you.' Dad said he'd try. He also promised to read more with Matthew, but that it was frustrating because Matthew read so poorly. I tried to tell him how important it was, and that by reading with him, he'd provide a very good role model."

Mrs. Schaefer had promised the parents she'd start working with Matthew in mid-March and that she'd continue to meet with him on a near-daily basis for the remainder of the school year. She hadn't explained the reason for the month-long delay: that for the time being, she needed to devote all her available time to the third, fourth, and fifth graders she had identified that year as having the potential, with an intensive nine weeks of her tutoring, to reach proficiency in language arts and, as a result, perhaps lift Brookside to a passing grade on the CMT.

The exam came and went. Over the next months, Mrs. Schaefer discovered she loved working with Matthew. He was sweet and eager and basked in her attention. "I was a little nervous, at first," Matthew said. "But when I got used to going to her room, I started to like her." The first books they had read together were *Dressed Up Sammy* and *Dilly Duck and Dally Duck*.

Together, they read two or three picture books a day, Mrs. Schaefer employing the same strategies she had taught Matthew's parents. At the end of each session, she placed the books in a bag to take home and reread with his mom and dad. Repetition—

reading familiar books over and over, she had explained to them—was key if a struggling reader were to gain confidence. Mrs. Gilroy was her partner in this process. Mrs. Schaefer advised her of the books they'd been reading, and the two met every few weeks to discuss Matthew's progress. "She told me how he was doing in small group instruction in the classroom, and what she thought we needed to work on with him, and I did the same for her," Mrs. Schaefer said. By the end of the school term, Matthew had begun to catch on. "Say there's a word, *elephant*," he said, "and I couldn't read that word because I didn't know the strategy—how to split it up and find a word inside it that you know, like *ant*. Mrs. Schaefer taught me that, and how to sound it out."

In late May, Mrs. Schaefer had tested Matthew again. He had improved to Level 10. Not great, still a half year below grade level, but a clear sign of progress. Together with Matthew, she assembled a summer reading list and handed it to his mother, placing stars beside Matthew's favorites. All were geared to Level 10—*Beep Beep, Bubble Trouble, The Fox and the Red Hen, Ten Bears in My Bed*, and more. "I can't emphasize enough how important it is that Matthew continues reading. It's the only way he'll continue to progress," she told Matthew's mother. In addition, Mrs. Schaefer provided her with a list of helpful websites for emerging or struggling readers. When Mrs. Schaefer learned Matthew had been assigned to Mrs. Walker for second grade, she'd had high hopes for him. But her hopes didn't last.

"The first day of school," Mrs. Walker said, "Matthew stood outside our classroom door and cried for at least an hour. He would not come in. He was so frightened of something. He just froze and stood against the wall outside and said, 'I'm not going in.'"

Eventually Dr. Masone, the assistant principal, came down and stood in the hallway with Matthew, trying to calm him. Mrs. Walker joined them every ten minutes or so, leaving her teacher's aide in charge of the class. "I kept trying to encourage him," Mrs. Walker said. "I told him, 'Come on inside, Matthew, come meet your new friends. Come see the classroom.'" He didn't budge, wouldn't stop crying. "We're all nervous, Matthew," Mrs. Walker said, gently. "It's the first day. Even I'm nervous." It was ten o'clock before he finally entered the room.

Matthew's reading deficit was apparent from the start. "Some of his language arts skills were just so not beginning second grade," Mrs. Walker said. "He came in a level twelve, but he was more like a ten, not knowing a lot of sight words. He should have been an eighteen. I was very concerned." Part of the problem, she discovered, was that instead of sticking to his Level 12, just-right books, he had been tackling material several levels higher. At the school library, he insisted on checking out books that were beyond his ability. "So he could say, 'Look what I'm reading,'" Mrs. Walker said. Each day, Mrs. Walker sent him home with a bag of just-right books. But away from school, he read what he wanted. Matthew's parents, eager for their son to progress, had gone along with his choices, unaware of the harm those books were doing. It was not surprising that Matthew had trouble making sense of what he was trying to read. Soon he grew discouraged, and stalled. Mrs. Walker found her biggest task was to rebuild his confidence. With Mrs. Schaefer occupied training teachers in workshop instruction and chairing curriculum meetings, Mrs. Walker was pretty much on her own.

Now it was November. Mrs. Schaefer hadn't seen much of

Matthew since he had entered second grade. She had monitored his progress, but mostly from afar. Seeing him now, she thought, little in him had changed. The boy was still so needy. She wished she could work daily with him again. During their time together, Matthew had given her his every effort. Which was more than she could say for Marbella, with whom she would likely have to work, come January, instead. What a shame, Mrs. Schaefer thought. Matthew was far more deserving of her help. She had been sincere when she'd told Matthew she'd read with him as soon as she found time. But that day wouldn't come for months.

Chapter 5

December 2010

The noise inside Mr. Morey's classroom seemed to bubble up from everywhere, like the percolating sound from a dozen pots of coffee. Chandler whispered to Aajah, who was seated behind him. Carlos sneezed. Dennis tapped a pencil on his desk. Josh showed off the baby tooth he lost at lunch. Monica asked something of Sergio and seemed disappointed when all she got in return was a shrug. All were supposed to be focused on their fifteen minutes of in-class, silent reading. Mr. Morey couldn't believe the cacophony. The class's behavior was all the more incredible, he thought, considering Mr. Hay was standing beside him. The two had been working to reconnect Mr. Morey's laptop to the SMART Board, and had their backs to the class. It was as if they were apparitions, not really there at all.

"Monica, come here," Mr. Morey finally said, turning around.

The ten-year-old approached his desk.

"Do you have a question?" he asked her, loud enough for the class to hear.

"No, why?"

"Because I saw you asking Sergio a question. Maybe I can help."

Monica got the message and returned silently to her seat. The rest of the class grew quiet as well. Mr. Hay left, and Mr. Morey resumed working on his laptop. All was peaceful . . . for two minutes, when the chattering started anew. Aajah said something, and Monica giggled. The joke spread round the room.

Mr. Morey shook his head. Silly season had begun. The moment the calendar had flipped to December, the children's thoughts had turned to Christmas—to holiday concerts, class parties, special assemblies, vacation. He could sense their attention begin to wander, especially toward the end of the day. There was little Mr. Morey could do. At least he didn't have it as bad as Mrs. Bernstein, the music teacher. The poor woman, he thought. She had spent months rehearsing the fifth graders for the schoolwide holiday concert. That morning, all progress had stalled. After listening to them sleepwalk their way through "'Twas the Night Before Christmas," Mrs. Bernstein had finally exploded. "This is the worst-prepared class I've ever had!" she had shouted, her voice rising a full octave. "We have two days before our concert, and many of you still don't know the words. One of you doesn't even know the tune." The children had snuck furtive looks at one another, several of them stifling grins. When Mrs. Bernstein blew, she held nothing back. To the students, especially the boys, music class was different from math or language arts. It wasn't an academic subject, one that until they stepped onstage, they really had to care about.

Even then, it wouldn't matter much. There were no solos, making it impossible for the audience—their parents—to tell who knew the song and who did not. The situation had made Mrs. Bernstein very uncomfortable. It wasn't often she'd had to battle ten-year-olds for the upper hand.

The silly season infected everyone, even the best-behaved students. That afternoon, Mr. Morey brought a visitor to class—a former student of his who now attended the local community college. Mr. Morey asked her to describe the transition from elementary to middle school, to help prepare his students for the changed atmosphere they'd encounter the following fall. The children squirmed in their seats. To them, the young woman appeared adult-like, closer to Mr. Morey's generation than theirs. "You know, I had a lot of the same teachers you had," she said, attempting to connect with them. She rattled off several familiar names, then dove into her topic. For fifteen minutes, she addressed middle school issues large and small—homework, hallway lockers, teachers' expectations, the four minutes they would have following the end-of-period bell to reach their next class. "Any questions?" she asked, upon finishing.

There was just one. Prim little Jacky raised her hand. "In fourth grade, you had Mrs. Arnold?" she asked.

"Yes, I did," the young woman said.

"Did she fart in your class like she farted in ours?"

M rs. Schaefer didn't play the silly season game. She couldn't afford to. Christmas break was just two weeks away, and she had to finalize her CMT prep groups by then. Her third- and fourth-grade selections were set. Her fifth-grade group, however, wasn't quite complete. She had already picked two students from Mrs. Keefe's class and three from Mrs. Bohrer's class. (Mrs. Bohrer had prevailed on her to take on an extra child whom Mrs. Bohrer adored.) Mrs. Schaefer had decided on Carlos as one of her choices from Mr. Morey's class. But her final selection—Marbella or Hydea?—remained up in the air. Since October, she had been meeting every week or so with Mr. Morey, comparing their work output as well as their attitude. The girls were so close in ability, it seemed to make little difference which one she chose. But Mrs. Schaefer remained haunted by that one year when Brookside came within a single student of passing the CMT. "I just felt I couldn't afford to make a mistake," she said.

Mrs. Schaefer was still leaning toward Marbella. Like Hydea, she had advanced to Level 38 at the start of the school year, meaning she was a beginning fourth-grade reader. Grade level was within her reach. All it would require, Mrs. Schaefer believed, was a few months of concentrated effort. That was the key. She wondered whether she could coax nine straight weeks of prep work out of Marbella, and then two additional weeks of effort during exams. One point in Marbella's favor was Mrs. Schaefer's track record with her family. Mrs. Schaefer had worked with Maryrose, Marbella's older sister, in her Reading Recovery program. "Maryrose struggled terribly in first grade, and in twenty weeks she reached proficiency," she said. "Maybe that's why I felt I could do the same thing for Marbella." Maryrose, though, had been a very different type of student. She had wanted to read better and had put forth great effort to improve. Everything Mrs. Schaefer knew about Marbella suggested otherwise.

Mrs. Schaefer thought back to the first time she had worked with Marbella, near the end of first grade. She had been nothing like the social butterfly she was now. Mrs. Schaefer had done some checking with Miss Samuel, Marbella's first-grade teacher, and found the girl had barely made a peep. That was a bit unusual for so late in the year. "It's maybe November or December when you start to see their true personalities," Miss Samuel explained one morning, seated at her classroom desk. "By February a lot of them start to blossom." Not Marbella. "She was very unsure of herself, academically and socially," the teacher said. "She relied on other students. During reading, I normally group three students together, with the strongest student in the middle. Marbella was always on the outside. She was already far behind." Back then, Marbella hadn't liked going to school. "I was scared," she recalled. "I was scared of people I didn't know and maybe they wouldn't like me."

Mrs. Schaefer had worked with her on fluency and comprehension, one-on-one and in small, in-class groups, through third grade. She had found the process frustrating. She would work with Marbella intensively, see improvement and return her to her classroom—where, invariably, Marbella would cease working hard and see her gains slip away. Mrs. Schaefer had always found Marbella sweet and cooperative. The child always did her work and had never complained. But Mrs. Schaefer sensed something missing in her. In all their time working together, "I never saw that *extra*," she said. "You know, there are some kids, when they get something or they feel really good about themselves, you can see it. You can see it in their eyes, you can see it in their face, that they just really feel they've accomplished something. I never saw that with Marbella. She just went through the motions. Even when she seemed to get it, it seemed like it didn't really matter to her. I got her into summer school to see if that might help her. But nothing got that internal motivation going."

Marbella's second- and third-grade teachers had noticed the same thing. Mrs. Canal, her second-grade teacher, worried that her reading difficulties were eroding her overall confidence. She fell behind not just in language arts but in math, science, and social studies as well. "I didn't find that she didn't want to read; it was that she was having trouble reading," Mrs. Canal recalled. "Sometimes when children feel that frustration of not being able to read, it can turn into lack of interest in reading." Mrs. Henneghan, Marbella's third-grade teacher, remembered how hard it was getting her to read a picture book from start to finish. "It was a struggle. Oh, my God, it was a struggle," she said. "[Marbella] would try. She wasn't the type of student that just sat and did nothing. With some kids, their self-esteem is kind of diminished a little bit. She knew she was reading below grade level. In third grade, she was on a second-grade level. A lot of times her homework came back and many of the answers were incorrect."

All the teachers believed Marbella's parents wanted the best for their daughter and were concerned about her progress. They attended class events and took seriously the reading tips the teachers gave them at parent-teacher conferences, to use when reading with Marbella at home. But the teachers weren't certain how much one-on-one time they actually devoted to her. Marbella's parents led busy lives. Her father's landscaping business demanded long hours, and her mother managed four daughters, two dogs, a part-time job, school, and a busy home. Afternoons, while cooking, her mother tried to help Marbella with her homework. But she couldn't oversee everything. Mrs. Schaefer thought it might have helped if she and her husband had attended her quarterly evening teach-ins over the years on how parents can improve their children's literacy. At parent-teacher conferences, Mrs. Canal remembered asking Marbella's mother to help Marbella with the books and sight words she sent home with her each day. "I think she and her husband wanted to," Mrs. Canal said. "I just feel, maybe with their lifestyle and their family, that they weren't able to give her the full support to help with her needs." Mrs. Henneghan had the impression that Marbella's parents had tried to help her but weren't always successful. On more than one occasion, she said, Marbella's parents had mentioned how much easier it had been for them working with their older daughters. "Sometimes it's not good to compare kids," Mrs. Henneghan had cautioned them, adding. "All of us are different."

To Mrs. Schaefer, though, Marbella's struggles resulted from more than a matter of ability. She questioned Marbella's attitude and maturity. Sometimes she believed that all Marbella truly cared about was getting by, that she lacked the internal drive to do more. Mrs. Schaefer was sufficiently concerned to phone her mother. The two spoke a number of times. "I told her mother that lots of times when I worked with her, she just acted silly," Mrs. Schaefer said. "Her mother just kind of passed it off, saying, 'That's Marbella, that's what she's like,' almost like it was cute. It wasn't so cute as she started getting older. She really needed to start taking more responsibility for herself." Then in fourth grade, matters for Marbella turned worse.

Marbella had trouble with the teacher. So did a number of her classmates, including Carlos, Chandler, and Aajah. The teacher, unable to manage them, repeatedly lost control of the room. By then, Marbella had emerged from her shell. Overnight, it seemed, she had grown incredibly social. In class, she was chatty, even giggly. She drew close to the two rambunctious boys, to Aajah (who said of her, "I like Marbella because she laughs weird, and I sort of like people that are weird, because I think they are interesting") and, by the end of the year, to Hydea. She began to speak her mind to other children, sometimes unkindly. She got into name-calling tiffs with girls in the bathroom, and more than once was sent to the office. She grew lax with her schoolwork—"The kids had to read fifteen to twenty pages a night. Marbella read nine pages, seven pages, and she was never reading what she was supposed to be reading," the teacher complained. Her grades slipped and her reading progress stalled. Mrs. Schaefer saw less of Marbella that year; by then, her job had changed from working with individual students to mentoring and monitoring their teachers. On the occasions when she visited Marbella's class, she was struck by how the girl had changed. "It's almost like having lots of friends and being part of the class seemed to be much more important to her than the academic side," she said.

Marbella didn't disagree. In third grade, she said, she sat by herself in class and drew pictures when she grew bored. In fourth grade, she put away her pencil and started yakking, mainly to Aajah and, toward the end of the year, to Hydea. Her attention flagged. Often, she didn't complete her homework. She knew she was falling further and further behind. When asked if that had bothered her, she answered, "Not really." Her parents didn't know what to do. Her mother, anxious for Marbella to complete her work, told her it would be all right if she handed it in a day late. At the end of the year, to no one's surprise, the teacher assigned her to summer school. Mrs. Schaefer approved; she thought the extra reading time could only help. Marbella, she knew, wouldn't read on her own. (Marbella had had a library card since age six, but had rarely used it. She told anyone who asked that she read only for school, never for pleasure. "She'll go in the library," her mother said, "and she'll look at a book and she'll go, 'Ooh, I like this book,' and look at it real quick, and then she's like, 'Okay, I'm done.' She will not come out of there with anything.") But Marbella missed a few critical weeks when her family went on vacation. *Typical,* Mrs. Schaefer had thought. She was somewhat surprised when Marbella returned to school and tested at Level 38, higher than she'd expected. Mrs. Schaefer was torn. Marbella was doing better. Perhaps something had finally clicked during her short time in summer school. Mr. Morey seemed to confirm that when, a few weeks into the school year, he had buttonholed her in the hallway and remarked on how hard Marbella had been working. Uncomfortable as Mrs. Schaefer felt placing her trust in Marbella, she believed the ten-year-old now had a reasonable chance of passing the CMT. *I'll probably end up taking her on,* she thought.

H ydea liked where she sat in Mr. Morey's class. Her desk was toward the front of the room, but off to the side, out of Mr. Morey's direct line of vision. If he couldn't see her, she thought, he might not call on her—especially in math or to explain anything that had to do with reading. She wanted to remain as anonymous as possible. That wasn't easy, given her height. For someone as shy as she, it had long been her curse.

From the start of first grade, Hydea had known she was slow at reading. Mrs. Roman, her second-grade teacher, thought she might have gotten a late start associating sounds with letters, making it difficult to combine them into syllables and words. In class, she expended so much effort decoding words, she had little mental energy left to group them into meaning. Even as she grew competent at decoding, her comprehension lagged behind. At home, she'd read to her grandma—read beautifully—without Grandma suspecting she barely understood a thing on the page. Grandma never quizzed her on comprehension, and Hydea seldom requested help. "I guess I didn't want to bother her," Hydea said.

She didn't want to bother her teachers, either. Twice a week in second grade, Hydea arrived at school at 8:30 A.M., half an hour before the school buses, to work with Mrs. Roman on letter sounds, sight words, and chunk sounds (*th* in *think*, for instance). Beyond that, it was up to Mrs. Roman to recognize when she needed help. "She would never say, 'Mrs. Roman, this is very difficult for me,' or, 'Mrs. Roman, I don't get it,'" the teacher said. Miss Sutton, her third-grade teacher, noticed the same thing. "Hydea sat in the middle of the room, just trying to blend in," she said. "She didn't want to bring attention to herself. That would have killed her, if something happened and I singled her out. When she came to me, she didn't have basic math skills—addition, subtraction, place value, telling time. But she wouldn't raise her hand and say, 'I need help.' She wouldn't say boo. You had to make sure you pulled her into a small math group, because she would never let you know she was struggling." At home, too, she had tried to figure out the process on her own. Only occasionally had she sought help from her grandma or older sister, because she hadn't wanted them to know, either. In fourth grade, nothing changed. "She would never raise her hand," her teacher said. "When I called on her directly, sometimes she wouldn't answer, because if students wanted, I had a rule where I allowed them to pass." About the only time Hydea was vocal was around Mother's Day, or when a classmate mentioned her mom. "She was very sensitive about her [late] mother," Mrs. Roman said. "She had several meltdowns."

By the time Hydea entered Mr. Morey's class, she was set in her ways, comfortable with her classroom persona. She felt content to let questions and answers and class discussions swirl about her, while she remained silent. Sometimes, Hydea confessed, she understood what Mr. Morey was explaining and sometimes she didn't, but she was okay with that. Somehow, she had convinced herself he was unaware of her continuing problems with multiplication and division—and, more recently, with fractions and beginning algebra. When asked early in the year why she didn't go to Mr. Morey for help—a teacher, she told her grandma, whom she adored—she had answered, "Because I'm not used to him."

Lately, though, Hydea had been begun to question herself. Sometimes she did know the answer to one of Mr. Morey's questions. Why shouldn't she raise her hand, she thought. She knew the reason: She was too lacking in confidence. Anyway, the smart kids, like Josh or Kyle, were almost always quicker than her with the right response, and she was just uncertain enough to let them claim the glory. Still, she wondered how it would feel, just once, to raise her hand and be brave. Only in Rabia did she brim with confidence, she thought.

It was her grandma who finally convinced her to try. One November afternoon, Grandma returned home from a parent-teacher conference with Mr. Morey and sat Hydea down in the living room. She showed Hydea her report card. "It said I wasn't where I should be on the reading, and that I should be with the fifth-grade level," Hydea said. "I looked at it and I saw what I was doing wrong." Her grandma said that Mr. Morey wanted her to participate in class more, that it would help her in every subject, not just language arts and math. "He wants you to gain confidence so you can be where you should be," her grandma said. Hydea, like Marbella, dreamed of being a veterinarian, a profession, she knew, that required a college degree. It meant a lot that Mr. Morey believed that much in her. She decided to take a chance in class—to read more and to participate. "I wanted to be up where other people were," she said.

Hydea's courage didn't come instantly. Almost a month passed before she saw her opportunity. Of all things, it came during a math lesson. Mr. Morey stood at the whiteboard, explaining how to add decimals. He wrote:

$$1.8$$
$$+\,2.4$$

"Who knows the answer?" he asked.

You have to try, Hydea told herself. You have to try. She raised her hand. She pulled it back down. Then she raised it again.

"Hydea?" Mr. Morey asked.

She answered incorrectly. Mr. Morey tried to reassure her, but it wasn't necessary. For once, Hydea wasn't discouraged. "At least I tried," she said. "I felt good that I tried."

A few days later during math period, she raised her hand again.

"The question was nine times nine, which is eighty-one," Hydea said. "At first I was kind of nervous to see if I knew the answer, and then I was happy when I did." Afterward, during snack time, Aajah raced up to her.

"You raised your hand!" she exclaimed.

"Yeah, finally. It's about time," Hydea said, grinning. Mr. Morey watched from his desk, trying to hide his pleasure as the girls hugged.

Chandler sat in his bedroom, doing some serious thinking. It wasn't like he had a choice. Earlier that day, he had talked back to Mr. Morey, and the teacher had sent him to the office. Before he reached Mr. Hay, though, Mr. Morey had fetched him back, saying he had a better idea. He phoned Chandler's mother. This was a chance, he told her, to turn Chandler around. Chandler's mother agreed. That night when his dad arrived home from work, father and son had a long talk. "He told me how it's not right, the way I was behaving, and we pay for you to go to school, and by acting up, it's just a waste of money," Chandler said. He couldn't argue with his father's logic. "I realized that if I kept being bad, then no one would like me," he said. "Not that many people would talk to me too much if I was a troublemaker, because if they talked to me, they could get in trouble, too." He mentioned his friend Kyle. "I like him," Chandler said, "and I saw his face a couple of times when I did something bad. It was like he didn't understand why I'd do something like that, and I thought, I guess I got to change my ways."

A few days later, Chandler saw his chance. The class had returned from the cafeteria before Mr. Morey's return from home. Every student knew what was expected of them: fifteen minutes of silent reading. With no teacher present, though, chatter erupted. Carlos started giggling. Chris reached into his desk for one of his action toys. Fernando made animal sounds. The noise built. Chandler, who sat near the door, heard Mr. Morey coming down the hall. "Let's get out our nonfiction books," he called to the class. The children faced Chandler. They saw he was serious. Immediately, everyone—even Carlos—settled down. By the time Mr. Morey entered the room, all the students were reading.

Chandler couldn't believe it—the whole class had listened, just as Mr. Morey had predicted a few weeks before. To Chandler, it was like he was a real leader, the first time he had experienced it outside of sports. Before the week was out, Carlos spoke to him privately about changing, too. Chandler was certain that he'd turned a corner. He even told his parents about it. Then a few days later, briefly, he lost it again. This time without being asked, he apologized to Mr. Morey. "I guess I'm going to have to keep working on controlling myself, because people say in middle school the teacher's not going to deal with that. I hope by the end of the year I'll be a new person," Chandler said.

Mrs. Bernstein wasn't taking any chances with the holiday concert. Over the years, the fifth graders had always been the stars of the show, the closing act. But this group—frankly, the music teacher wasn't sure she could trust them. She was made even more nervous by their attire. Usually, the children wore their Sunday best on performance day. After all, their parents and grandparents would be in the audience. But as the teachers lined them up in the hallway by height, boys on one side and the girls on the other, she noticed several wearing T-shirts or jeans. She decided she had been wise to make them the opening act, and close with the fourth graders, instead.

The children filed into the gymnasium and climbed the risers onstage. Mrs. Bernstein stood below them, beside her piano on the gym floor. The crowd welcomed them with polite applause. The teacher led the fifth graders through "Ode to Joy," which they played haltingly on their recorders, followed by "Festival of Lights," "The Light of Kwanzaa," and "The Christmas Tree Feud," the last of which had been planned as their signature number. Mrs. Bernstein had arranged it so it the boys and girls alternated verses, and sang the chorus together. The girls sang beautifully. All would have been fine, had the boys sung on key. But this was silly season. Several still hadn't learned the words or their parts. More than a few felt guilty. As the children filed offstage, Edwin, one of Mrs. Bohrer's students, offered the pithiest review. His mother, he knew, had closed her hair-styling shop to see him sing. "Without the girls," he said, "it would have been a disaster."

It was time for Mrs. Schaefer to reach a decision on Marbella and Hydea. The teacher was still conflicted. She didn't trust Marbella, yet she hadn't seen the breakthrough she had hoped for with Hydea. In her team meetings with the fifth-grade teachers, she had been emphasizing a portion of the CMT called Degrees of Reading Power (DRP), an exercise that tests both reading comprehension and vocabulary. The test asks students to read a series of short, nonfiction passages, each peppered with blank spaces that they must fill with the most appropriate word among five choices. Historically, Brookside students had performed poorly on the DRP. Mr. Hay believed, and Mrs. Schaefer agreed, that the root cause was a lack of exposure to nonfiction vocabulary at home—meaning an absence of newspapers, nonfiction books, and news magazines. That morning, Mr. Morey announced he had found a collection of DRP practice tests on Study Island, an education website. Mrs. Schaefer decided to stop by his room, to see how his students fared. It would provide a perfect opportunity, she thought, to observe the two girls at work. Dr. Masone, the assistant principal, accompanied her.

Mr. Morey fired up his laptop, hit a few keys and "Passage A" appeared on the SMART Board. The first paragraph read:

> During the days of the American Revolution, women
> as well as men fought for freedom. Many women
> actively supported the patriot side when war broke
> out. That is how they showed they
> were _____.

The choices were as follows:

A. cruel
B. foolish
C. weak

D. loyal

E. reckless

Mrs. Schaefer ambled to Marbella's desk from behind, and peeked over her shoulder so as not to disturb her. It was clear the ten-year-old was unsure of the answer. She scribbled C, erased it, changed her mind, entered C again. Mrs. Schaefer grew concerned. It seemed to her Marbella wasn't concentrating, that she had hurried through the paragraph just to get the exercise over with. She stepped from behind the girl's desk and stood beside her. "Marbella," Mrs. Schaefer said, "I want you to read that paragraph over again, but this time out loud. I want you to take your time and use the same word to fill in the blank."

This did not thrill Marbella, who, in fact, *did* want to get the exercise over with. She glanced up at Mrs. Schaefer, wondering why she was being singled out, and soldiered through the three sentences again.

"What do you think about the word *weak*?" she asked. "Do you think it makes sense here?"

Marbella shrugged. Finally, she said no. But she made no move to read the paragraph a third time and choose a new answer. It seemed to Mrs. Schaefer that she didn't much care. The literacy specialist tried again. "It's okay, Marbella," she said. "The whole idea of this is practice, and the more you practice, the better you get. The important thing is that you just don't pick any old answer, that you really think the problem through and you choose the one that makes the most sense." Mrs. Schaefer enumerated the strategies Mr. Morey had been teaching: Reread when you get stuck.

Try out each word choice, till you find the one that works best in context. Eliminate words that obviously don't fit. She encouraged Marbella to try yet again, then left her side and continued her stroll around the classroom. Mrs. Schaefer never changed expression, never let on to the girl how discouraged she was by her lack of effort. In truth, Mrs. Schaefer had run out of patience. She thought, *There are more than five hundred children in this school, I'm the only literacy specialist, and I have time these next nine weeks to work personally with just eighteen of them. I have to pick the ones who are most deserving.* Before she reached Mr. Morey's desk, she made her first decision: Marbella was out of her special tutoring group. Mrs. Schaefer felt terrible about it. She exited the classroom feeling as though it were she who somehow had failed. "Usually I'm pretty good about finding some way inside of students to motivate them, and I guess I just haven't found it with Marbella," Mrs. Schaefer said later, in her office. "I haven't truly made a difference with her."

That left Hydea. Mrs. Schaefer still had doubts about her. It was true Hydea had scored not merely "proficient" or "goal" but "advanced" on the writing portion of her fourth-grade CMT. But Mrs. Schaefer considered that misleading. It didn't correspond to her CMT reading score, reading level, or history of achievement at Brookside. Yes, Hydea had progressed in summer school, but was she capable of more? The literacy specialist had never worked with the girl individually, so she didn't know her all that well. She discounted Hydea's fourth-grade struggles; she was confident Mr. Morey could bring out the best in the ten-year-old. To Mrs. Schaefer, the biggest factor in Hydea's favor was her attitude. In summer school, she had displayed determination and had boosted her reading score. That had been a good sign. Attitude was important to Mrs. Schaefer. Early in the year, when Mr. Morey had reported that Hydea was making strides in language arts, Mrs. Schaefer had been pleased. Still, she had decided to wait and see. She wanted more evidence that Hydea was ready to move to the next level. Several times since, she had gone to Mr. Morey's room and asked to see Hydea's writing. Mr. Morey's assessment, she decided, had been a bit exaggerated. Her November story on Charlie DeLeo had been somewhat garbled. Not when she explained it to me orally, Mr. Morey had insisted. Mrs. Schaefer had been noncommittal. She needed more proof.

Now, in December, Mr. Morey called Mrs. Schaefer back to his room. "She's raising her hand in class," he said. "She's reading more. She's at the same level as Marbella. I want you to look at her latest paper." Mr. Morey had assigned a passage on Sandra Day O'Connor—a three-page story that explained how, through persistence, perseverance, and applied intelligence, O'Connor had risen in an era when even educated women were often limited professionally, to become America's first female Supreme Court justice.

"I came into Mr. Morey's room, and he was having a conference with Hydea on her paper," Mrs. Schaefer said. She stood behind them, leaning over their shoulders. "They were talking about the main idea of the story," she said. "Just listening to their conversation, for Hydea, it was almost like, 'Oh yeah, I understand now. I can do it.' She was so close. It was at that point that I thought, why wouldn't I take her? Here's a kid who really wants to do better."

Back in her office, Mrs. Schaefer grew all the more certain of her decision. It was no secret among the faculty that the girl was insecure. Most considered it her greatest impediment. The literacy specialist thought, In a small group, where the two of us can meet every day and build a relationship, where Hydea comes to know I care about her, she just might be able to overcome her inner doubts. If she does, she'll have a chance to reach proficiency.

The next afternoon, after telling Mr. Morey of her plans, she stopped Hydea in the hallway outside her office, as Hydea waited in line to board her school bus home. "I've got some good news," she chirped. "I've chosen you for my special class!" Mrs. Schaefer thought Hydea would be pleased, even excited. But initially, the ten-year-old was unenthusiastic. "I told her okay," Hydea said, "but in my head I really didn't understand why. I didn't want to leave my class." It wasn't till she talked to her grandma and Mr. Morey that she agreed to give it a try.

Mrs. Bernstein did not give in easily. As she had for the last three years, she booked the fifth graders to perform their holiday show at the Norwalk Senior Center. She was determined to wring one solid performance from them. She rehearsed the children till they finally knew their parts. A week before Christmas vacation, the students dressed in their best clothes (well, all but one or two), boarded two yellow school buses, and drove across town with Mrs. Bernstein and their teachers.

The center, a sprawling, redbrick building, reminded the children of a middle school: off-white cinder-block walls, scuffed linoleum, hallways similar to Brookside's, only bigger. In a way, it felt familiar to them. They lined up again by sex and height, and trooped onto a stage equipped with risers. Instead of a gymnasium, they were in a cafeteria that doubled as a performance hall. Their audience was roughly two hundred grandmas and grandpas, all dressed in clothes the colors of Christmas, seated at picnic-style tables festooned with red and green ribbons.

Mrs. Bernstein sat at a piano on the cafeteria floor. She played the opening notes to "The Light of Kwanzaa," the children's best number from the Brookside concert, and with a nod of her head the fifth graders began to sing. In turn, they followed with "Festival of Lights" and "Para Pedir Posada," a Spanish lullaby. Each song earned polite applause. "The Christmas Tree Feud" went a little better this time, the boys singing on key. The audience swayed in their seats. Still, they weren't truly engaged. They whispered throughout the performance and fiddled with their party favors. Even the finale, a "'Twas the Night Before Christmas" sing-along, lacked spirit. The seniors' talk grew louder. Some made like they were ready to leave. The children stood quietly onstage, not knowing quite what to do.

Hydea, who missed her mother and missed her father, who was ever thankful for her beloved grandma, didn't want the day to end like that. Standing tall in the back row of singers, resplendent in her red turtleneck and black jeans, a red hair band highlighting her dark brown hair, she flashed an enormous smile and waved to the crowd. She wouldn't stop. Soon, her classmates were waving. And then all the grandmas and grandpas waved back. The holiday spirit swept over them all. To Hydea, to her classmates, to Mrs. Bernstein and the teachers, to the seniors in the audience, it truly felt like Christmas.

Afterward, Hydea had a hard time explaining why she'd started in. "I just thought it would be nice," she said. She couldn't wait to tell her grandma. She had never done anything like that before. The memory of it stayed with her the rest of the day. Maybe this really was the start of something new, she thought. Not that she was eager for vacation to pass and school to restart, but she was anxious to see what January would bring.

Chapter 6

Grandma. Mrs. Schaefer luxuriated in the word, let it roll off her tongue. Her daughter-in-law—also a literacy specialist— had just given birth to a baby girl, and grandma was home with her, helping care for the newborn and new mom. Mrs. Schaefer had anticipated this moment for four years, ever since her son's marriage. For much of this first week of January, Brookside had seemed far away. She peeked into the baby's bedroom. Books already filled the room. In time, she knew, she would help teach the child to read. In that moment, the thought of school came rushing back. It reminded her—as if she needed reminding—that there were eighteen Brookside children, six each from her special third-, fourth-, and fifth-grade CMT prep classes, who needed her care as well. A whole week of work was being lost. Mrs. Schaefer felt sick about it. *If only I could have those days back,* she thought.

Mr. Morey was all business, a message he wanted to convey to his students. The first morning back in school, he rose from his desk and walked to the front of the room. "Boys and girls," he said, "now that vacation's over, it's time to get to work." He spread his arms wide and shrugged. "That's the way of the world," he said. "You're just like everyone else."

Mr. Morey plowed ahead. He had a lot of ground to cover this morning and limited time. "The CMT is in March. We have two months to get ready for it, and that's what we're going to do," he said. There were a few isolated groans. Mr. Morey placed his hands on his hips. This class needed a wake-up call more than most. He posed three rhetorical questions and answered them all. "Is the CMT important? Yes. Is it the end of the world? No. Do I want you to take it seriously? Yes. Every fifth grader in America," he continued, "takes some version of the CMT, and every fifth grader in Connecticut takes the same test you will." The exams, he said, would tell them where they stood compared to their class-mates, their grade, their town, their state, and where Brookside stood, as well. "I don't want you to stress," he said, "but I do want the best out of you. If you're not giving me your best, I'm going to get on you just like a football coach. You might succeed, you might fail, but I want you to ask yourselves, are you giving your best? And if you're not, you know what you have to do."

His last sentence captured the attention of all the students, even Fernando and Dennis. Seldom had they seen Mr. Morey so intent, except when he was yelling at them. Silly season was definitely over. They wondered if he was going to be like this the rest of the year. It didn't seem like a whole lot of fun.

Mr. Morey circled the room and handed each student a thick, green-and-white CMT language arts study guide, similar in form to what high school students use to prepare for the SAT. "This is the book we're going to be studying from," he said. A few flipped through the pages; most let it lay on their desk. To them, it was just another textbook. Mr. Morey told them to open it to the table of contents. Together they read the headings: "Part 1—Reading Comprehension," "Part 2—Degrees of Reading Power," "Part 3—Editing and Revising." "Those are the three skills you're going to be tested on," he said. "Let's go to 'Part 1, Chapter One, The Meaning of Words.'" Mr. Morey slapped the book cover. "Now we get going. Now we get into it." He pivoted, and on the whiteboard he wrote:

> **Point of view**
> **Simile**
> **Metaphor**
> **Personification**
> **Onomatopoeia**
> **Imagery**
> **Humor**

For the next hour, the students reviewed the use of literary devices. They broke ten minutes for snack time, then went back to work, this time on vocabulary. They had eight new words to learn: *capable*, *emanate*, *distinguish*, *tendency*, *detect*, *mundane*, *revelation*, and *elicit*. Each appeared in a *Time for Kids* article on zoologists

Mr. Morey had assigned. After they had finished transcribing the words and definitions in their vocabulary notebooks, Mr. Morey called their attention to the whiteboard. Upon it he had printed, *Reading Goals for 2011*. "I want each of you to think of a weakness you have in reading, and make improving it your goal," he said. "Think about it a minute, and then turn to the person next to you and share your goal." It was a strategy he had learned from Mrs. Schaefer, part of the workshop program: Children, she had explained, are more apt to learn when they make their own choices. Mrs. Schaefer wished he and the other fifth-grade teachers would heed it more.

"Tell me what you came up with," Mr. Morey said, after giving them a few minutes to confer.

"Hydea says she wants to understand better what she's reading," Marbella said. Sara piped up, "I said the same thing."

"That's reading comprehension," Mr. Morey said.

Leo raised his hand. "Reading for a longer time," he volunteered.

"That's reading stamina," the teacher said.

Mr. Morey called on each student, then said, "Good, you all have a goal. Now, how are you going to accomplish it?" Shrugs all around. The teacher plopped on the rug and called the students to him, in groups of four. Fernando was first. His goal, he said was to "stop reading choppy." Mr. Morey, aware that his parents spoke little English and could not help with any of his homework, suggested he read aloud to his second-grade sister. "You argue a lot with her. Read to her, instead," he said. He told Carlos, who was easily distracted and short on reading stamina, that for independent reading, he would move him to an isolated desk in the front of the room. "That way, you're going to really have to work if you want to turn around and look at someone." To Hydea, he said, "If you want to get better at comprehension, you can always reread. Another way is to make connections between the story and your own life. Maybe you read about what one of the characters does, and you go, 'This reminds me of when I did this.' That's something I do. Sometimes I make three or four connections on a single page." He advised Chandler, whose problem was staying focused, "You need to choose books that interest you. If you're really into a book, it will hold your attention."

Mr. Morey sent the children back to their desks, with instructions to write their goal and how they proposed to achieve it in their workshop journals. It took them till lunchtime. Two thirds of the day was gone. Upon their return, the students spent fifteen minutes on independent reading and an hour on math, before switching back to language arts. They finished the day listing and describing as many nonfiction genres as they could. There had been no time for other subjects. Not a minute for social studies or science.

To the students, Mr. Morey had been extraordinarily businesslike, not the laid-back teacher they'd known since September—the one who liked to go off on tangents and talk about famous World War II battles or growing up in Staten Island or whether LeBron James could hold a candle to Michael Jordan. That day, Mr. Morey hadn't tolerated any nonsense. When Fernando had cracked a silly joke, he had jumped all over him. Mr. Morey had covered a ton of material, more than the children were used to, more than some of them could digest. Walking to her locker at the end of the day, Hydea said it was hard to keep up when things moved so fast, hard to even think about raising her hand.

Mr. Morey, in fact, was in a hurry. He wanted to plow through the reading comprehension section as efficiently as possible to devote additional time to DRP. That morning, during the fifth-grade teachers' weekly language arts lesson-planning meeting, Dr. Masone (she was sitting in for Mrs. Schaefer, who was absent that day) had projected a summary of their students' CMT reading scores from the previous year on a whiteboard. The news wasn't good. Slightly more than a third had fallen short of proficiency, meaning the school had failed in that category by a wide margin. Dr. Masone had emphasized a single point: "Our weakest link on reading was DRP, and DRP counts for fifty percent of the CMT reading score." When at one juncture, Mr. Morey, Mrs. Bohrer, and Mrs. Keefe debated how much time they should devote to teaching the components of a fiction story, Dr. Masone had reiterated, "If you want more bang for your buck, DRP is where you can go."

It was a message Mr. Hay and Mrs. Schaefer had been trying to sell to the faculty since the fall of 2007, after that year's CMT scores had come in. That spring, more than 48 percent of the fourth graders, 35 percent of the third graders, and 32 percent of the fifth graders had failed the CMT reading portion—among the lowest scores in Norwalk. "I remember Linda came to my office at the start of the [2007–08] school year," Mr. Hay said. "We were half a year from the 2008 CMT, but we both had a pretty good sense of what the scores would be. She sat down in a chair and said, 'We're not getting better, we're not moving. What can we do?'"

Together, they crunched numbers, trying to find patterns, hints, anything in the scores. In four of the five areas of literacy, they found, their students were performing relatively well. Then they came to the DRP section. "We were getting killed, every year," Mr. Hay said. "We realized, this is what's holding us back."

Mr. Hay was well aware how few students had newspapers, news magazines, or nonfiction books in their homes. It struck him that nonfiction material was in short supply at Brookside, as well. "Basal readers contained mostly fiction," he said. "And though we had moved away from the basal approach, we kept buying fiction [for the classroom and school libraries]. It was out of tradition, I guess." He went to Mrs. Madden and instructed her to spend the next several years beefing up the library's nonfiction collection. He allotted each teacher $300 to purchase nonfiction books for their classroom library. Finally, together with Mrs. Schaefer in 2008, he initiated a professional development program for the faculty on how to teach nonfiction.

It didn't help. Brookside's failing rate in reading continued to top 30 percent. Mrs. Schaefer decided to examine the second grade's DRP scores. They turned out to be the worst in the city. "One day," Mr. Hay said, "I was talking to Mrs. Roman," a second-grade teacher. "She said that all the fiction books in her classroom library were leveled"—in other words, rated according to their reading difficulty, so she could place them in the right student's hands—"but her nonfiction books weren't. It was another thing we had to address."

Mr. Hay realized he had to change the curriculum, too, placing far more emphasis on nonfiction reading than he had before. That meant reeducating the faculty, many of them veterans reluctant to adjust their teaching. "I don't think they were anti," Mr. Hay said, "but if you've been teaching for years and have had some success, you ask, 'Why do I need to change?' What I was asking was pretty drastic—to go from using 90 percent fiction material to 50 percent. To go from teaching social studies to a combination of social studies and literacy. We're still working on it." Mrs. Schaefer grew so frustrated with the holdouts, she pressed Mr. Hay to pay unannounced, pop-in visits to their classrooms to watch them teach. Mr. Morey was one of the first faculty members to embrace their plan. Mr. Hay and Mrs. Schaefer were hopeful his class would make a qualitative leap this year, and that other teachers would take note and adjust their own styles accordingly.

Unfortunately for them both, Mr. Morey was called for jury duty—a personal injury case. He would miss more than a week of class. Each day, he left a detailed schedule for the substitute to follow. The schedules were virtually the same—day-long attention to CMT subjects, at the expense of all else, the only changes being chorus, art, or music in place of gym:

9:00–9:30—Arrival and morning work (crossword puzzles, math games, etc.)

9:30–10:00—DRP practice

10:00–10:26—Vocabulary

10:26–10:56—CMT prep (identify main idea and cite two supporting details from text)

10:56–11:15—Snack

11:15–12:15—Computer lab (research time for their reports on one of the thirteen colonies—the only time set aside that day for a non-CMT subject)

12:15–12:40—Math (review improper fractions)

12:40–1:00—Recess

1:00–1:30—Lunch

1:30–2:15—Reading (focus on nonfiction genres)

2:15–2:30—Read aloud to the class (from the book
   Cirque du Freak)

2:30–2:45—Clear desks, pack up

2:45–3:15—Gym

3:15–3:25—Dismissal

Mr. Morey wasn't optimistic about how, in his absence, his class would behave. He fully expected the children to test the substitute and quickly overwhelm her. The first day, the sub left him a withering report. Each day thereafter, the news was the same. Carlos, Fernando, Dennis, Marbella, Chandler (he had backslid)— they had all caused a ruckus or refused to do their work. Mr. Morey shook his head. Chandler's behavior, in particular, disappointed him. Worse, a week of CMT prep had been lost that he wasn't certain they could make up. He thought he had been on the cusp of turning this group around. *Of all the luck,* he thought.

Hydea was in a rare cloudy mood. It was the day of the annual school science fair, and she was embarrassed to show her project. She wished Mr. Morey were here, but he was still on jury duty. Mr. Morey was nice, the kind of teacher who might have given her an extra day to redo her presentation. But the way things stood, she had no choice. The substitute teacher had already lined up the class; in a minute they'd march to the gym, where they'd assemble their projects.

The students cradled their work in their arms. Some had boxes filled with scientific apparatus: test tubes, batteries, coloring agents, and the like. Others lugged large, tri-paneled display boards, on which they described, in neat handwriting (that smacked of parental assistance), the methodology behind their experiment. It was a day for the smart kids, a day for a student such as Josh, who, having recently visited the dentist, had wondered about the acid present in everyday beverages and its effect on tooth decay. First, using litmus paper, he had measured the acidity in a variety of drinks, including Sprite, Coke, apple juice, tap water, bottled water, and milk. Next he had poured each into a glass containing a chicken bone. Over a period of thirty-six hours, he photographed the damage to the various chicken bones. Coke had proved the most acidic, while Sprite had triggered the greatest decay. The least acidic beverages were tap water and milk. Josh noted he could have improved the quality of his experiment by isolating the acids from other substances in the beverages, such as sugars, sodium, and additives. He labeled each of the ruined bones and placed them on display. He would go on to win a blue ribbon for presenting the best experiment among all of Norwalk's fifth graders. The district office had made a commitment to improving science education, and the annual science fair was its public face.

Hydea's experiment wasn't in the same league. She knew she wasn't the best science student; still, she had wanted to do a good job. Experiments were the one aspect of science she liked—the possibility of seeing magic happen before her eyes. Since early December she had surfed the Internet, trying to find a fun experiment to replicate. Her older sister, Billi, suggested feeding water mixed with food coloring to a variety of houseplants, to see if they changed hue. But Hydea worried it would take too long. She considered a project on outer space, but decided it was too much work. In the end, she decided to repeat her fourth-grade science fair project. She would demonstrate how, through a chemical reaction, she could create an egg that bounced. "I forgot how it worked, so my grandma said it was okay if I did it again," Hydea said. She went online and searched for the ingredients and instructions.

All she needed was a hard-boiled egg, a large bowl, a bottle of white vinegar, and patience. She submerged the egg in a bowlful of vinegar and waited a week for the egg shell to dissolve. What remained was a rubbery orb that bounced like a ball. The experiment had worked beautifully . . . except for the egg's acrid odor. Hydea soaked it in water overnight, hoping to wash away the smell. Meanwhile, she transcribed her findings onto a poster board. The school district had distributed a handout on scientific method, enumerating the seven steps the students were to follow when conducting an experiment. The procedure was clear: Pose a question. Perform background research. Construct a hypothesis. Test with an experiment. Analyze the results and draw a conclusion. State whether the hypothesis was true, partially true, or false. Report the results. Hydea, who misplaced her handout, forgot about steps one, two, three, five, and six. Across the top of her poster board, she printed in large, halting letters, How to Bounce a Egg. Beneath it were a series of time-lapse drawings illustrating the various stages of her metamorphosing egg, tracing its journey from raw to bouncy. Farther down, she described the experiment's three steps.

Hydea wanted to bring the egg to school, but she didn't dare. The odor remained, and she was certain her classmates would make fun of her. Worse, virtually all the students—in fact, almost the entire fifth grade—had prepared elaborate, tri-paneled display boards to accompany their work. "My project was just words on a piece of paper, and a picture of eggs," she said. As inconspicuously as she could, she placed her poster board on a display table and slipped away. "I wish I had done better," she said. In that moment, all her newfound confidence seemed to evaporate.

At least Hydea had tried. Three of Mrs. Bohrer's students had ignored the assignment. "You're not off the hook here," the teacher informed them. She asked for ideas on experiments they might try. The three had no idea what to do. Mrs. Bohrer wasn't about to give in. "I'm going to come up with a project for each of you." She mentioned the class would study outer space next. "The moon and the sun!" she enthused. "Who would like to do something on that?"

No one raised a hand.

"How about this?" Mrs. Bohrer asked, trying again. "I have Play-Doh. You can make a demonstration project on the planets in relation to the sun. How many of you would like that?"

No response.

"I'm thinking about a science project on animals," she said, trying a different tact. "How many of you like animals?"

Again, no response.

"What about the constellations in the sky? Were the stars important to the [fifteenth- and sixteenth-century] explorers we studied?"

Shrugs all around.

"Did they help the explorers navigate?"

One girl nodded affirmatively.

"Maybe you can draw pictures of the constellations. Are you interested?"

All shook their heads, no.

"Well, the three of you are going to have to find something," Mrs. Bohrer said firmly, struggling to retain the upper hand. She sent the girls back to their desks. *To be continued,* she thought.

M rs. Schaefer didn't beat around the bush. At 10:30 Monday morning, she shut the door to her office and addressed the six fifth graders she had selected for her daily CMT prep group. They sat in two groups of three, boys at one table, girls at another. It was the second week of winter semester, Mrs. Schaefer's first day back at school. She saw from the children's expressions that they had no idea why they had been pulled from class. "The reason the six of you are with me," she explained, in a gentle voice meant to put them at ease, "is because I took a look at your CMT scores from last year and felt that each of you was right on the cusp of really getting it. You did okay, but your teachers and I think you can be better. Working with you in a small group, I think that will help you." The children—two from Mrs. Keefe's class, two from Mrs. Bohrer's class (a third from Mrs. Bohrer's class would eventually join the group) and Carlos and Hydea—listened politely, but showed no reaction. Mrs. Schaefer tried again. "I need every single student at Brookside to do their best on the CMT," she said, "and the idea of this class is so you feel so comfortable with the material that there will be no surprises on the test." The students still weren't clear why they'd been singled out.

Half an hour was all Mrs. Schaefer had with them. Five of her thirty minutes were already gone. She felt she had no more time to waste. She distributed copies of a two-page passage on the healthful benefits of cranberries, and had the students read it. Another five minutes passed.

"When I ask, 'What's the main idea?' what am I asking for?" she inquired.

"What the paragraph is mostly about," one of Mrs. Keefe's students replied.

Mrs. Schaefer uncapped a marker, unfurled a large sheet of paper over an easel, and on it wrote:

Passage
Paragraph

"What's the difference between these two?" she asked. No one raised a hand. Mrs. Schaefer was certain they all knew the answer. At least, she hoped they did. They were terms they'd learned in second grade. Perhaps the children were still unnerved to be in her class. "A passage is the whole story," she reminded them. "A paragraph is one part of the passage." She made them repeat the definitions aloud. "Okay now," Mrs. Schaefer said. "Carlos, what's the main idea of the passage?"

"That cranberries are delicious and healthy," he replied.

"I couldn't have said it better myself," Mrs. Schaefer said. "The author used four supporting details to make his point," she continued. "I want everyone to find them in the passage and write them down." Mrs. Schaefer circled the two tables, peering over the students' shoulders to check their answers. Carlos had simply restated the main idea. Hydea had jotted down one detail and then stopped.

"Do you know all four, Hydea?" Mrs. Schaefer asked.

"I think," she said, uncertainly.

"You think! What can you do when you're not sure about something you've read?"

"Read it again?" Hydea asked.

She's remembered one of the strategies for improving her comprehension, the teacher thought. Mrs. Schaefer saw an opportunity to turn the moment into a positive. "What Hydea said is so smart," she said, smiling at Hydea and addressing the class. "Rereading is what we do when we get lost or stuck or don't understand." She scanned the room. The children were listening, but she wasn't sure they were absorbing. Mrs. Schaefer returned to the easel. "I want you to hold up your right hand," Mrs. Schaefer directed the students. "I want you to imagine that your palm is the main idea. Your fingers are the supporting details." She had the children reread the passage. "Every time you come to a supporting detail, I want you to underline it," she said. By the time the children finished the exercise, their half hour was up. *This isn't going to be easy,* Mrs. Schaefer thought.

After the students filed from her room, Mrs. Schaefer sat at her desk and replayed the session in her head. Only Kevin, one of Mrs. Bohrer's students, had seemed to grasp the lesson, and even he had rushed through the passages and made careless mistakes. Mrs. Schaefer faced a formidable challenge: She had to lift four of the six to proficiency, and the same in grades three and four, if Brookside was to have any hope of passing the CMT. She was particularly worried about Hydea. From the hesitant way she had answered in class, the girl seemed almost devoid of self-esteem.

Self-esteem, Hydea would have told her, was the least of her concerns. Hydea liked Mrs. Schaefer, but felt unnerved sitting in her room. In that small space, it seemed like a million eyes were on her. If only Hydea could explain it to her. "I don't want to be there," she told a friend, on her way back to Mr. Morey's class. It had taken her months to grow comfortable with Mr. Morey, to ease her reticence, and now it was like she had to start all over again.

Mrs. Schaefer's next few days with the class went no better. One morning Mrs. Schaefer handed out a fresh two-page passage, this one on the mysteries of Saturn and how it differs from Earth. It began,

> *Stewart has been learning about the planets in his fifth-grade class.*
> *He reads this article about Saturn, the planet that interests him most.*

"What's this article about?" Mrs. Schaefer asked, from her seat at the girls' table.

Kevin raised his hand. "It's about a boy who is interested in space," he said.

"Not in space. Don't assume information that isn't there," Mrs. Schaefer said. "He's interested in planets, especially Saturn. Hydea, what do the [boldface] headings at the top of each paragraph tell you?"

Hydea shifted uncomfortably. This was the primary reason she wanted to return to Mr. Morey's room. In a class of twenty-two (early in the school year, a new student had joined them), she was less likely to be called on.

"What the passage is about?" she guessed.

"What the passage is about, or what the paragraph is about?" Mrs. Schaefer asked.

Hydea ducked her head. "Paragraph," she mumbled, embarrassed. She had feared the other students might make fun of her, but none did. After Mrs. Schaefer distributed a page of multiple-choice questions based on the Saturn passage—a page similar to what they'd find on the CMT—she realized the others were having problems of their own. One question in particular had stumped them all. "What is the section of the article called 'Life as We Know It' mainly about?" it asked. There were four choices given, and between the six students they picked all four. Patiently, Mrs. Schaefer suggested to them, "Go back and read the first sentence, the topic sentence. The topic sentence will tell you the answer."

It wasn't the students' low level of achievement that concerned Mrs. Schaefer. She was used to that. Low achievers were the only students she saw. It was the arbitrariness of it all. Why Hydea and not, say, Sergio, also from Mr. Morey's class, a sweet, serious-minded boy she had tutored from first grade through third, but who had no chance of passing the CMT? Didn't he deserve her attention, too? The first and second graders weren't the only needy students who missed out on her services during those nine prep weeks, from the first week of January to the first week of March.

Sergio. He was a puzzle his teachers and Mrs. Schaefer had thus far been unable to solve. He was bright in math and always completed his homework. He was popular with classmates, who considered him funny. He never misbehaved. He had good role models at home. His older brother and sister had attended Brookside, where they were remembered as conscientious students and grade-level readers. Both currently attended the local community college. Already, his brother had progressed further in school than either of his parents. Yet Sergio had stumbled from the start. He read robotically, possessed a third grader's vocabulary, had poor reading comprehension, lacked grammar skills, had difficulty decoding words, and had trouble organizing his thoughts on paper.

Over the years, Mrs. Schaefer had come to know something of Sergio and his family. He was the youngest of three, born to Honduran parents who had emigrated to the United States in 1995, in hope of bettering their lives. "That was our goal," Sergio's father said. "To come to the United State, thinking that our children could find better opportunities here, find better job." But where Sergio's siblings had been self-motivated, Sergio required help. He couldn't always find it, for reasons that were beyond his control. His father, a school-bus driver in neighboring Wilton, Connecticut, was conversant in English and could read and write the language, but was uncertain when teaching his son. Sergio's mother, who spoke just a few words of English, couldn't help him at all. His siblings worked with Sergio when they could. But between college classes and part-time jobs, they were seldom home. Mrs. Schaefer knew how badly Sergio wanted to improve his reading. Earlier in the year, he had approached a school volunteer and asked if he could practice reading aloud to him. She had been deeply touched. "We always say, grades K through two, you're teaching kids to read," Mrs. Schaefer said. "Once they hit grade three, they're reading to learn information. But not everyone has that foundation by grade three." Sergio was one who did not. "It's a shame," Mrs. Schaefer continued, "but there aren't the resources here for me to help every child. I'm one person, and at some point, I have to make choices. Between data that we had, my observations and the teachers' observations on which kids they felt had the most chance of moving up, I had to leave Sergio out. I could help him, but not enough to reach proficiency on the CMT."

Mrs. Schaefer shook her head. Just saying those words caused her discomfort. Many times Mr. Hay had told her, had told all the faculty, "Our job is to move every child forward. If we can do that, I'm not worried how we score on the CMT." Yet when push came to shove, with all the pressure to achieve from the district, the state, the U.S. Department of Education and the media (but not the students' parents; almost all were happy with the school), another side of Mr. Hay and Mrs. Schaefer emerged. The two would scroll through reams of computer printouts, staring at the glow of data on their computer screens, searching for any edge that might help Brookside pass the exam.

The calendar read January 24, but to Mr. Morey it seemed almost like the first day of school. He had spent more than a week away on jury duty, and at last his court case was over. "I missed you all," he told his students, and following the morning announcements, he called them to the rug in the front of the room. He pulled up a chair, stretched out his legs. He was dressed in a pullover shirt, cargo pants, and sneakers—not all that different from the clothes his students wore. "I want to tell you about the trial, because it made me think of you," he said.

He explained the case to them: A woman with cerebral palsy had sued her landlord for $80,000 after falling on blacktop in front of her duplex and breaking her leg. She claimed the blacktop hadn't been adequately cleared of snow and that the thin remaining layer had turned, after melting and refreezing, to black ice. "There were six of us on the jury," he told the students. "We all felt so sorry for the woman. We wanted to award her the money. But then we heard the evidence."

The woman said she fell at 4:30 P.M. on February 10, 2004. There had been a six-inch snowfall four days earlier. The landlord produced bills proving the blacktop had been plowed. The woman claimed the blacktop had later iced over, and the landlord had done nothing to make it safe. At that point the landlord's lawyer called a meteorologist to the stand. The meteorologist, citing National Weather Service hourly temperature readings from that day, testified it was fifty degrees at the time the woman fell.

"As bad as we felt for her," Mr. Morey said, "we decided that the landlord was not guilty. At fifty degrees, there couldn't have been black ice. He didn't have to pay her." Mr. Morey paused a moment, then continued. "It made me think of you guys, because it served as a good reminder: When you're reading a nonfiction piece or writing about one on the CMT, it's not enough to identify the main theme. You have to find examples in the story that support it. Just like a jury, you have to have proof."

Mr. Morey liked teaching in parables. Deliver a lesson through an engaging story, he believed, and students will remember it. He'd need plenty more. The CMTs were now six weeks away. There was an enormous amount of material to cover, and so much time had frittered away.

All Mr. Morey's fears concerning his class had proved true. The students had accomplished almost nothing during his absence. While on jury duty, he had missed several team meetings with Mrs. Schaefer and the other fifth-grade teachers, placing him a bit out of the loop on test-prep strategy. On top of that, six days had been lost to record snows—so many, that the superintendent would cancel the district's annual, one-week winter vacation in part to salvage some CMT study time. His students were hopelessly behind. They scored poorly on a DRP practice test. In math, more than a few still needed their fingers to negotiate the times tables. Some had yet to master basic punctuation, such as placing a period at the end of a sentence or using a capital letter at the start of a new one. What chance did he stand of catching them up? What might the consequences be for Brookside if he didn't?

One news story had struck home. *The Connecticut Post*, the county's largest newspaper, reported that the Bridgeport school board had voted to request that the state take over its public school system, after its most recent superintendent had failed to raise the city's test scores, which ranked as the worst in the state. If it happened, all the district's teachers would be in jeopardy. Could they all be so inept? Did they all deserve to be fired? A friend told a story of his colleague, Mrs. Sweeters, a Brookside second-grade teacher. She had received her first job offer from a Bridgeport elementary school. The school shared space with a middle school in a tough city neighborhood. Mrs. Sweeters, slender and earnest, had recently earned her teaching certificate. "Listen to me carefully," the principal had told her, after escorting her through the forbidding building. "I'm offering you a job. I'm advising you not to take it." It made Mr. Morey stop and think. He was one of Brookside's most popular teachers. Parents lobbied to place their children in his class. He served on the district's math steering committee. He had one Fernando. Big and tall as he was, what if he taught in a school like the one Mrs. Sweeters had applied to, and had seven or eight Fernandos? Could he control them all? Could he teach effectively? There was no certainty he could even get his current Brookside class to pass the CMT.

More and more, he had been thinking what his career would

have been like had he remained in Redding, the wealthy suburb where he had done his student teaching. He hadn't encountered any Fernandos there. And yet, there had been a number of subpar students. He had tutored several when he had needed extra money. That had been a key difference, he decided: Redding parents, by and large well educated, who stressed the importance of education to their children, had the means to address their childrens' problems. Long ago, Mr. Morey had established his teaching style. Like every teacher, his was indelible, unique, like a fingerprint. Would he be judged more harshly, more favorably, he wondered, in Bridgeport, in Redding?

No time for that now. He placed his musings aside. He had a class to teach. After being away so long, he was anxious to begin.

Mr. Morey had had days to plan his first lesson, on narrative elements in fiction. He had decided to teach it not through a book, but through *iCarly*, a Nickelodeon TV show popular with ten-year-olds. Thanks to his own young children, he was familiar with all their favorite TV programs, music, movies, and books. Speaking their language gave him credibility. It was one of the reasons the children considered him cool.

"Most of you are reading fiction from the library," he said. "You're reading for enjoyment, maybe to escape. It's the same reason you watch *iCarly*. You follow the characters around, and they do silly things. [Seventeen-year-old Carly and her best friends, Sam and Freddie, produce their own webcast in Carly's Seattle apartment.] You like the characters, you like the plot, you like the setting. Is the setting important?" he asked, rhetorically. "Yes. The show takes place in her apartment, in the present tense."

Mr. Morey prodded the students to recall some of their favorite episodes. Kyle mentioned the time when someone opened a smelly bottle in the studio, and Carly and the crew were forced to evacuate and run downstairs. Aajah brought up the team's trip to Japan.

"Carly's bossy," Sara said.

"I think she's mean," said Marbella.

"If you understand the characters, the plot, and the setting, how can it help you while you watch the show or when you read?" Mr. Morey asked.

No one raised a hand.

"What are you reading now?" he asked Sara. Sara pulled out a copy of *Stargirl*, by Jerry Spinelli, the story of a teenager who enters the local high school after years of being homeschooled. Marbella was reading it, too.

"If we know enough about our characters, we can predict what's going to happen to them," Mr. Morey said. "Sara, can you give me Stargirl's personality traits?"

"Well, she's tall," Sara said.

"That's a physical trait," he corrected.

"Okay, she's smart because she always reads books and she studies all the time."

"Stop right there," Mr. Morey said. "You gave me a personality trait and then you proved it—she's smart because she always reads and studies. That's perfect."

Marbella mentioned that Kevin attends Stargirl's school.

"What is one of Kevin's personality traits?" Mr. Morey asked.

Marbella shook her head. She was stuck. Mr. Morey decided to go at the question another way. He believed that Marbella learned best not through books, but through personal experience. "How would you describe your personality?" he asked. *If she can do that,* he thought, *she'll probably understand what I'm getting at.*

"I don't know," she said.

"I'll help you out," Mr. Morey said. "You're very outgoing, you have lots of friends, you love going to Block Island in the summer. So when you read the book, try to figure out what the characters are like. Is Stargirl outgoing, like you? Think about those kinds of things, because it affects the plot, what the story's about."

Mr. Morey walked to the whiteboard in the rear of the room, and started to write their homework assignments. In mid-word, he stopped himself and faced the class. He wanted to drive home the good job Sara had done. "What Sara said, when she was describing Stargirl's character traits, that was so smart," he repeated, nodding toward her. "She gave her main trait—that she's smart—and she backed it up, saying she read and studied. That's what smart people do."

It was a wonderful lesson, a deeply satisfying one, Mr. Morey thought, turning back to the whiteboard. Then Dennis piped up. "I don't study, so I guess I'm not smart," he said, trying for a laugh. Mr. Morey faced around and quickly stepped in. "You're smart. I think you're smart, Dennis," he said. "But maybe you're not as smart as your potential. You're probably naturally good at soccer [Dennis played for a community team], but if you practiced, you could be great. Saying you're smart and you don't study is nothing to be proud of. Think about that." He was quite certain Dennis wouldn't think about it at all.

Dennis. Mr. Morey found him exhausting. Every day, the same impudent remarks, the disinclination to listen or do classwork. Mr.

Morey had tried for months to reach him. The boy was indeed bright, self-aware enough to convince his parents to hire him a math tutor. But now Mr. Morey was fed up. And not just with Dennis, he realized. He was tired of dealing with Fernando and his inability to pay attention, with Carlos raising his hand to go to the bathroom in the middle of a lesson he didn't understand, with Chandler's recent backward slide from class leader to class clown. He had had it with them. The next morning, he walked to the front of the room and addressed the class.

"There are some of you who don't care about your education or anybody else's," he said, speaking quietly. "Whatever group you're in, you bring down their work." He ticked off the troublemakers' names. "I'm going to be honest—I really don't like teaching right now, because I know I care more about your education than you do. You think it's all right to laugh, and you don't care if you disrupt the education of those who want to study. You think it's funny. I tell you, my job would be so much easier if I didn't care. I'd just go ahead and go through the lessons and you could learn, or not. But I do. The way some of you are acting, you're going to have trouble getting through high school. It used to be, you could graduate from high school and get a good job. Today a high school degree won't get you anything like that. A high school degree will get you a job flipping burgers at McDonald's." He shook his head, hoping his message had gotten through, knowing it probably hadn't. "Okay, let's get to work," he said. On the whiteboard he wrote a single word: *waterfall*. "I want you to write a story based on that word. You have to incorporate it somehow. It can be through setting, plot, metaphor—any narrative element. That's your challenge."

The children went to work. All except Dennis, who looked around the room, fiddled with an empty piece of paper, and then yawned. When Dennis realized his seatmates were ignoring him, he picked up a pencil. But he just held it. Dennis, Mr. Morey knew, was sending a message. No one could tell him what to do. His page remained blank.

Marbella loved wearing new clothes, and on this bitterly cold January day, she had come to school in a stylish black jacket she had gotten for Christmas. Even so, she was in a prickly mood. Today was Thursday, and each Thursday (and Wednesday) found her stuck after school in Mrs. Keefe's supplemental reading group. Her mother had enrolled her in the class at Mr. Morey's suggestion. It wasn't the daily, intensive tutoring she would have gotten from Mrs. Schaefer, but Mr. Morey had assured her it was the next best thing—that it would improve Marbella's reading comprehension and better prepare her for the CMT.

Marbella's mother knew reading comprehension was her daughter's weak point. Since first grade, every teacher had said the same thing. So far, none of their strategies had worked. But "Keep trying" was Marbella's mom's motto. Marbella had taken a similar class from Mrs. Keefe in fourth grade, and for a while her reading and writing had improved. She hadn't liked doing the work—she had had to be prodded to expend effort—but she had enjoyed Mrs. Keefe, and because Mrs. Keefe had taught her older sisters, the teacher had devoted extra time to her. Not surprisingly, when her after-school sessions with Mrs. Keefe had ended and the trouble in her regular classroom had escalated, Marbella had stalled.

Now, a year later, Marbella was back in the same classroom, repeating the same types of reading and writing exercises. She wasn't any happier being there than Hydea was in hers. At least Hydea didn't have to stay after school, she thought. Twice a week, Marbella had to sit for an hour with five other fifth graders—one of them Fernando—reading passages from the CMT workbook, and then answering questions about them, or worse, having to write a whole page on some related topic. Like it wasn't enough that she had to spend hours every day in Mr. Morey's class doing the same thing, studying DRP and reading comprehension, fiction and nonfiction, plot and character, theme and summary, forever reading and writing, then rereading and rewriting, till she just wanted to go home and blast a Justin Bieber CD and forget about everything.

Marbella was too self-absorbed to realize the others were trying their best—even Fernando, who, for all his tomfoolery, knew his poor reading was holding him back. In fact, he had begged Mrs. Schaefer—not once, but twice—for a spot in the class. But Marbella just couldn't get excited about it. She was certain Mrs. Keefe was testing them on the same passages they had covered the year before. Some days, she felt as though she had been sent back to fourth grade.

One February morning, Marbella stopped one of the girls from Mrs. Keefe's group in the hallway. "I'm not coming anymore. Tell Mrs. Keefe," she said. When the girl asked why, Marbella said she had better things to do. Mrs. Keefe was disappointed when she heard. Mr. Morey grimaced. "Her mother approved?" he asked, surprised. In fact, her mother went a month without knowing. She assumed the sessions had ended. Marbella never told her otherwise.

The fifth-grade teachers were gathered in the conference room in the main office, awaiting Mrs. Schaefer. There was none of the usual banter. The CMT was less than three weeks away.

Mrs. Keefe got straight to the point when the literacy specialist walked in. The day before, she said, she had given her students another in a series of DRP exercises. One passage, from the CMT workbook, had centered on a Kentucky coal mine. Her students, weak on nonfiction to begin with and unfamiliar with mining, had fared terribly. "My kids were so depressed when they learned their scores, I let them take the test home so they could try to figure out where they went wrong," Mrs. Keefe said.

"Did they try all the strategies? Rereading, trying to place words in context, eliminating the multiple-choice options that are clearly incorrect?" Mrs. Schaefer asked.

"How do you prepare a student for a passage where they have zero background and no knowledge?" Mrs. Bohrer asked. "Some of my kids didn't even finish the test."

All three looked to Mrs. Schaefer for guidance. "Let's not cry about it," Mrs. Schaefer said, not wanting this to turn into a pity party. She searched for something, anything positive. "What were our strengths?" she asked.

"The majority of the students were able to master fourth-grade requirements," Mrs. Keefe said.

"What does that mean?" asked Mrs. Schaefer. "That they comprehended on a fourth-grade level, so the next step is to apply the same strategies to more difficult texts?"

"I don't think that's realistic," Mrs. Bohrer said. She went on. "The other night I was reading *Goodnight Moon* to my granddaughter, who's six and a half. I read her a rhyme about mush. She said, 'Oh, that's porridge.' No way any of our students would know porridge. They wouldn't know porridge if they sat in it."

"This goes back to the achievement gap," Mrs. Schaefer said.

"Ah, the achievement gap," piped Mr. Morey. "Everyone wants to blame the schools for the education gap. The place where you solve the education gap is at home. I say there's no education gap in homes where the parents have read to their children since they were babies, constantly exposing them to new vocabulary."

The teachers had veered off topic. "Look," said Mrs. Schaefer, adjusting her glasses, adopting a businesslike tone. "This isn't getting us anywhere. We have to come up with a plan for the test. My feeling is, have your students focus on the first DRP passages, the easier ones. Remember, the graders count only the answers that are right. They don't penalize wrong ones. Tell your students that if they haven't finished and time is running out, just guess. Don't leave any questions blank. Just bubble something in. They have a one-in-five chance of picking a right answer. Some of them might get lucky. Who knows?

"One more thing," she continued. "With so little time left before the test, [you] have to identify those who are close to being proficient. I hate to say this, and I sympathize with the kids who aren't close, but right now [you] have to concentrate on the kids [you] can help and let the rest do the best they can."

The man most responsible for the CMT is a compact, bespectacled gentleman named Gerald Tirozzi, who from 1983 to 1991 served as Connecticut's commissioner of education. For twenty years, he had worked for the New Haven (Connecticut) United School District, first as a middle school teacher, later as a principal, finally as its school superintendent. Poor, urban, largely African American, the district was one of the most troubled in the state. Tirozzi's six-year tenure there as superintendent, beginning in 1977, had been difficult. State funding was short, teacher salaries were low, the dropout rate high. He came to the state commissioner's post with an agenda in mind: to level the playing field between the wealthy, white suburban districts flush with property tax income to lavish on their schools, and the cash-starved urban and rural districts, including New Haven, that had to scuffle for every dollar. To do so, Tirozzi would have to win over the state legislature, and 165 autonomous school districts that had little history of working together. It helped that *Sheff v. O'Neill*, a case alleging inequities in the state's city and suburban school districts, was then making its way through the state courts. For a man looking for a mandate, he couldn't have had better timing. "I was appointed the very same day the U.S. Department of Education released 'A Nation at Risk,'" the 1983 national call to arms to revitalize public education, Tirozzi said. "The very same day. It called for higher standards, for kids to take more academic subjects, et cetera. It turned out to be a great catalyst. The [Connecticut] general assembly was really poised for someone to come forward and say, let's do things differently."

On Tirozzi's staff, serving in the Bureau of Research, Evaluation, and Student Assessment department, was a driven researcher named Doug Rindone. Part of Rindone's job was to analyze standardized test data throughout the state. It proved a frustrating task. The available data were overly broad and thus of little use, and varied from district to district. The state, for instance, required testing in three grades from third to eighth, but did not specify which grades. Some districts tested third, fifth, and seventh graders; others, fourth, sixth, and eighth. Nor did the state create its own tests. School districts were left to select from what was commercially available; most used either the Iowa Test of Basic Skills or the Metropolitan Achievement Tests. Many of their questions did not conform to state curricula. It wasn't till 1979 that Connecticut, as part of a growing, nationwide movement toward developing minimum, grade-by-grade achievement standards, created its own exam, this one for ninth graders, called the Proficiency Test. Its purpose was decidedly modest: to identify whether students had the minimum academic skills to advance through high school. "We purposely set it where most kids were going to pass," Rindone said. Roughly 80 percent did. Aside from identifying, in Rindone's words, "the bottom students who were going to need extra help," it had little value.

Rindone, aware that Tirozzi favored a system of much earlier and more comprehensive student assessments, drafted a brief on what such a test might look like. He recommended that the bar be set high to enforce a high level of achievement. Tirozzi agreed. He assigned a team from the student assessment division to draw up the test. The result—implemented in October 1985—was the CMT, the Connecticut Mastery Test, issued to the state's fourth, sixth, and eighth graders. "The key word," Tirozzi said, "was *mastery*. We didn't call it proficiency. We did a lot of work around the state consulting committees of teachers, parents, school superintendents, and school board members on what kids should be able to do and know in core subjects. Not proficiency, but when you left fourth grade, what should you know?

"We always saw [the test] as a self-improvement model. The purpose," he emphasized, "was never to punish. It was to bring daylight to what kids in Connecticut were doing. We never broke it down by individual student. It was, 'As a district, this is where you are. How do you get better?' The goal, ideally, was to close the gap between the richest and poorest kids."

Initially, not every community bought into the test. "Places like Greenwich and New Canaan and Westport"—among the wealthiest and least diverse towns in the state—"laughed at us, because they said the state could never come up with a test that their kids could not master," Tirozzi said. "And lo and behold, the first results came out and they scored almost as low as the cities. It was almost embarrassing for them. We disaggregated the data. We broke the scores down by race, by gender, by type of community. We insisted that every school have a report card. We thought parents deserved to know how their children, and how their children's schools, were doing." Tirozzi was most proud of a $300 million teacher reform initiative he pushed through the state legislature in 1986, in which 90 percent of the money set aside for increased teacher salaries went to Connecticut's poorer urban and rural school districts. "For the first time, they were in position to compete for teachers like they never were before," he said.

Throughout the 1990s, the CMT worked as well as Tirozzi and

his colleagues had hoped. Each year, the U.S. Department of Education administered a survey test to a nationwide sample of fourth, eighth, and twelfth graders, called the National Assessment of Education Progress, and Connecticut consistently ranked in the top tier among states—the result, Tirozzi said, of superior teachers and the high standards demanded by the CMT.

The burst of money brought quality teachers to the state. School superintendents remarked they never had had so many skilled candidates apply for jobs. "Teachers were leaving other states to come to Connecticut," Tirozzi said. They had to meet the state's new, stringent requirements: Teachers had to major in their teaching subject and had to pass a subject-level test before entering a classroom. (Elementary school teachers were tested in language arts and math.) New hires were issued a provisional, one-year teaching certificate, and during that year were observed by six tenured teachers from other school districts who had the power to overrule the superintendent regarding issuance of a permanent teaching certificate. A professional development program was implemented for teachers and principals, to provide cutting-edge training and to improve their overall classroom skills. They began to teach a more rigorous and focused curriculum, as demanded by the CMT.

State educators remember it as a golden era. Then, in rapid succession, the economy stagnated, causing the state education department's funding to slowly evaporate. Shortly after, Congress passed No Child Left Behind. Where mastery had been the Connecticut standard, proficiency, a significantly lower federal marker, took its place. Tirozzi, who left his commissioner's post in 1991 to become assistant secretary of education under President Bill Clinton, was appalled. "What has always been shocking to me is how the [federal agencies] have taken the word *proficiency* and translated it to mean 'grade level,'" he said. "There's no relationship whatsoever."

For a while, Connecticut tried to adhere to its own, higher standards. "The [state education] commissioner at the time, Theodore Sergi, reported two sets of numbers for a couple of years—here's what the feds are requiring, and here's what we think we should be reporting," recalled Peter Behuniak, a University of Connecticut educational psychology professor who was then a key member of the state department of education assessment team. But inevitably, over time, the federal benchmark took primacy. In 2005, in accordance with a new NCLB protocol (and despite a failed lawsuit filed by then–state Commissioner of Education Betty Sternberg, attempting, in part, to block it), CMT testing expanded in the elementary schools to include third and fifth graders. Previously, only fourth graders had been tested. That same year, the exam shifted from October to March. (The CMT is also issued to sixth, seventh, and eighth graders.)

Expanding the testing to include third and fifth graders had seemed a good idea, on the face of it. NCLB officials argued it would increase the data pool and make teachers and schools more accountable for their students' learning. But the issue had proved more complex than that. According to Behuniak, evidence suggested that student test scores tend not to change significantly in the space of a year. And, he said, there was the ever-present danger that additional testing would lead to increased test prep, at the expense of a well-balanced curriculum. Then he pointed to a third, hidden result. Behuniak and his colleagues believed a new class of students was being shortchanged: those who were above average or advanced. With so much of a school district's resources now devoted to lifting below-average students (and, by extension, its schools) to proficiency, little remained for the academically talented. "That's a different orientation than there had been previously," Behuniak said. In fact, it was the polar opposite. Instead of striving for student excellence, schools now pursued a level of achievement that, to hear Tirozzi describe it, was something less than mediocre.

Moving the test to March had altered the intent of the CMT almost as dramatically. The main thought had been to provide teachers with more time over the course of the school year to teach to the test, which educators agree can be a good thing, if done wisely. Strictly speaking, if the CMT is based on knowledge contained in a well-crafted curriculum, then mastery of that curriculum will result in a good score. (Teaching to the test to the exclusion of all other subjects, said Tirozzi, Rindone, and Behuniak, is where the problem lies.) It also addressed concerns about the entering third graders now required to take the test. Many educations believed they were too young and ill-prepared to begin the school year with such an exhaustive battery of tests.

Tirozzi and his staff were among those who agreed, which is why they favored withholding the CMT until fourth grade. But they advocated testing students in October. They had wanted the CMT to represent the sum of an elementary school student's knowledge at the start of the school year. That way, a student's score would reflect an arc of learning that placed responsibility equally on all his previous teachers, not just his current one. In fact, because the child's current teacher would have had him for only a month, she wouldn't bear much responsibility at all for his score. It would also relieve teachers of having to live under the undue pressure of test prep for six months. And since the scores would be announced in December, teachers would be able to analyze their students' strengths and weaknesses, and adjust their instruction accordingly.

Tirozzi had anticipated problems when NCLB altered the blueprint he and his colleagues had created. But he had not realized the extent to which it would, in his words, "cause people to start doing strange things when they teach."

"I've seen elementary schools have pep rallies around the tests to get the kids revved up," Tirozzi said, unaware that that had occurred at Brookside. He ticked off the cheating scandals that have tarnished Connecticut and other states and the increasingly common practice among schools to drop their regular curricula for two months to focus exclusively on NCLB test prep. "That's what NCLB has done to us," he said. "It's driven us to lower our standards to look better, and it's caused teachers and principals to act very differently than they normally would. If you want to keep your job, if you have a family to support, you'll do what you have to do. I'm not saying they should cheat. I'm saying they're doing things we could never imagine a few years ago."

Tirozzi wished to be clear. "Don't misunderstand me," he said. "I applaud this movement toward national standards. I think the nation is going to be awakened [when a truly rigorous national test is administered] because there are going to be a significant number of kids, even in our richest communities, that aren't going to look that good. And I think unless and until we raise those standards and we teach to those standards and we test to those standards, we're going to have trouble competing with other countries with higher standards."

Left unsaid was that the new, more challenging national standards test he anticipates would almost certainly result in the same types of pressures on educators, precipitating the same disturbing behaviors.

As soon as Mr. Morey said, "Boys and girls, get in your testing positions," Marbella knew she was in trouble. She dropped her head. Her pigtails sagged against the back of her neck. Mr. Morey was passing out a practice exam on editing and revising, a portion of the CMT that would count for 40 percent of their writing score, and she hadn't studied. Like much of the CMT, it was multiple choice: Read a poorly constructed passage, and then choose the most sensible correction from a list of five options. The students separated their desks from one another. Marbella knew Mr. Morey wanted them to do well. The real test was about two weeks away.

Immediately, everyone fell to work, even Dennis and Fernando. Josh was among the first to finish. He reviewed his answers and put down his pencil. Several others, included Marbella, finished soon after. When the last stragglers were done, Mr. Morey collected their papers and led the children down the hall to art class. He returned to his desk to grade their work. Marbella said a little prayer.

Mr. Morey read through Josh's exam. Josh had done a good

job, as expected, correctly answering thirty-four of the thirty-eight questions. Next he graded Marbella's. She had also gotten thirty-four right—and the same four, wrong. *That's odd,* Mr. Morey thought. He double-checked Josh's exam, just to make sure. Suspicious now, he examined their previous editing and revising exam, from a few weeks back. Once again, the same answers right, the identical ones wrong. Both times, Marbella had sat a few feet from Josh. Mr. Morey called Dr. Masone. Dr. Masone phoned Marbella's father and then called Marbella to her office.

When Marbella entered, she saw her father with Dr. Masone and Mr. Morey. Her father looked very disturbed. She knew she had been caught. Dr. Masone started talking. Why had she cheated? She should never have done that. If it happened again, Dr. Masone said, there would be serious consequences. Marbella had been in trouble before, but never like this.

Back home, things grew worse. It was one thing to disappoint Dr. Masone and Mr. Morey, but quite another to let down her parents. "Every time we tried to talk to her about it, she ran to the couch in the living room, and threw herself down and started crying," her mother said.

At first Marbella denied she had cheated. Her parents weren't buying it. "When you're upset," her mother told her, "it's because you are admitting what you did was wrong."

"No, no, no. I didn't do it," Marbella squealed and ran out of the room, insisting she had done nothing wrong. She cried for quite a while. Marbella's mother waited for her tears to subside, then approached her again. "Marbella," she gently said, "Be honest, don't lie. Just tell us: Did you do it?"

"Yeah, I did it," she admitted, between sobs.

Her mother let out a sigh. "Why?" she asked.

Marbella wouldn't say. "I don't know. I just copied his paper," she said. Later, she confessed to her sister Melanie, "Mr. Morey said the test was important, and I didn't study, so I copied off somebody."

Marbella cried herself into exhaustion; she slept through the afternoon and evening, till 8:00. Through tears, she promised her parents never to do anything like that again. The next day, Mr. Morey made her retake the test. This time, she answered eighteen correctly.

Aajah's mom pulled up outside Hydea's apartment a little after five P.M. on a frigid Saturday. Hydea skipped down her front walk and climbed into the backseat of the car. "Hi," she said to Aajah and Marbella, crowding up against them.

"Are you ready, girls?" Aajah's mom asked. She pulled away from the curb. Next stop, Sammy's Fish Box, an hour away in City Island, in the Bronx. It was Aajah's birthday celebration. She was eleven.

The girls wore knock-around clothes, the kind they'd wear around the house. They grew loud almost immediately; so loud Aajah's mom had to ask them to chill. Marbella presented Aajah with a T-shirt. Hydea gave her a gold necklace, from which hung a heart. Marbella then pulled out her iPod, and she and Aajah played Temple Run, an addictive, action video game in which players steal an idol from an ancient temple and must escape a demonic band of monkeys who want the idol, too. Hydea played on her Nintendo, waiting her turn. As she did, she thought about their friendship. She and Aajah had been best friends since kindergarten. They had a lot in common. Both had experienced loss. Aajah lived apart from her father, Hydea had lost her mom. Aajah and her mother were extremely close, just as Hydea was with her grandma. They both like the same music. Their current favorite was the rapper Trey Songz. To Hydea, the two of them just clicked.

Hydea's friendship with Marbella had been far less smooth. They had met in third grade but had not hit it off. "I was trying to be her friend, but she was rolling her eyes and stuff," Hydea recalled. "I just wanted another friend besides the same friends every time, but it didn't go so well." It was Aajah who in fourth grade had brought them all together. For a while, the three were inseparable. But lately, Hydea had the feeling that Marbella was competing with her for primacy with Aajah. The two of them talked on the phone constantly. Hydea felt left out. She had asked Aajah if they were still best friends, and though Aajah had assured her they were, Hydea was unconvinced. She was glad the three of them were together this night. Maybe, she thought, things would go back to being like they were before. She turned to the others and asked what they planned to eat. Hydea—the new, adventurous, no-longer-shy Hydea—had decided on lobster, a dish she had never tried.

Sammy's was boisterous and very crowded. Marbella ordered fish and chips. Aajah, like Hydea, ordered lobster. They donned the restaurant's goofy-looking lobster bibs, and played Temple Run while waiting for their meal. When the lobster platters arrived, the two girls had no idea what to do. Marbella volunteered to tutor them on the art of tearing off the claws. She demonstrated

on Aajah's lobster and to Hydea seemed quite accomplished . . .
until, to their horror, the claw squirted out of Marbella's hands.
Next thing they knew, it was lying on the floor. A grownup at the
next table stared at them. Hydea, thinking quickly, hid her lobster
and pointed to Aajah. Marbella hid her fish and did the same. The
grownup kept staring until Aajah left her seat and retrieved the
claw. Afterward, the three couldn't stop laughing. They were still
giggling an hour later when they piled into the car and headed
home. In minutes, all were fast asleep, splayed on top of one another like kittens. "That was the most fun time I ever had with
them," she told her grandma, when she arrived home. The girls
would never be that close again.

Chapter 7

Early March 2011

The Brookside gym was rocking. It was the Friday afternoon before the start of the CMT; the tests would run nine straight school days, beginning Monday. Mr. Hay stood in front of the stage, fiddling with a microphone as the school's third, fourth, and fifth graders paraded into the room, readying to pump up his students, just as he had at the preexam assembly the year before. Justin Bieber's latest single, the inspirational "Never Say Never," blasted over a boom box. Marbella—Mrs. Bieber, Aajah called her—entered the gym with her class, singing along and swaying to the beat.

Marbella did not make the connection between the song and the coming exams. It wasn't clear if any of the fifth graders did. Symbolism was one of the elements of fiction they'd studied, but few thought of it outside the context of their assigned reading.

Nonetheless, the CMTs weighed heavily on their minds. Sergio said his father told him every night, while helping him with his homework, "Read carefully. Do the best you can." Carlos wondered every day, at school and at home, if he'd learned enough to pull through. Hydea couldn't escape the thought of the CMT, even in her sleep. "Sometimes I dream I'm taking the test and doing really well, and then I take the last part and fail," she said.

As for Marbella, she told friends she hadn't given a thought to the exams. But that was just a pose. Ever since the cheating incident, she had turned diligent about her schoolwork. She returned home from class, ate a quick snack, and then climbed the stairs to her study alcove and went to work. She no longer had to be bribed to do so. Marbella's sisters wanted to believe she had been scared straight after being caught. But her changed attitude was only somewhat related to her cheating. Key was her mother's warning. "I told Marbella," her mother said, "you need to do well on the CMTs. If you fail, they're going to keep you back and you'll have to repeat fifth grade." That was the last thing she wanted.

The music faded. Marbella and her schoolmates watched as Mr. Hay, microphone in hand, walked to the VIP section the custodian had arranged near the stage, and introduced the ten special guests he had invited to Brookside: Mayor Moccia; three front-office representatives from the local minor-league baseball team, the Bridgeport Bluefish; the Norwalk police chief and deputy fire chief; a local Channel 12 news anchor/reporter; the Brien McMahon High School principal; State Senator Bob Duff; and U.S. Representative Jim Himes. The students paid scant attention. They were pooped. The three fifth-grade classes had spent all morning reviewing test-taking strategies and then applying them during a final, forty-five-minute CMT practice test on editing and revising—the first exam on the CMT schedule. One of Mrs. Bohrer's students had put down her pencil after answering the final question and laid her head on her desk.

So far, the children thought, it was not much of an assembly. There wasn't even a food table. At the conclusion of the festivities the year before, the teachers had handed everyone a big square of vanilla sheet cake. The students awaited the inevitable—the parade of exhortatory pre-CMT sales pitches from Mr. Hay and their teachers, the ones they heard every year at this time, saying how important it was for them to lay it on the line over the next two weeks for good old Brookside.

But the teachers never said a peep and Mr. Hay made no mention of the CMT. Instead, Mr. Hay scanned the room, merriment in his eyes, and bellowed into the microphone, "It's Dr. Seuss's birthday today!" At that moment, one of the author's beloved characters, the Lorax, bounded onstage, dressed in his signature, rust-red, floor-length smock. The Lorax twirled his yellow, walrus-style mustache and wiped his brows, which appeared to be made of pipe cleaners. He gestured to the wing of the stage. Thirty-seven Brookside students came tromping out—the cast of the school's spring musical, *Seussical Jr.* All wore matching, knee-length electric-blue-colored T-shirts with yellow lettering that shouted the name of their play. To their schoolmates' delight, and with the Lorax looking on, the actors belted out several numbers from their upcoming show. When the room quieted, the Lorax stepped to the foot of the stage. "Hi, everybody," he said. "Do we love to read at Brookside?"

Mr. Hay took the microphone and explained the Lorax's presence: In honor of Dr. Seuss, Brookside, together with thousands of schools nationwide, was celebrating Read Across America (an annual reading awareness program sponsored by the National Education Association). "The way we're going to do that is to read—all of us—as many books as we can," he said. He challenged them: "So far this year, all of you, together, have read four thousand thirty-one books. Our goal is ten thousand. Think we can do it?" The children applauded, stomped their feet. The literacy specialist based at the district office then entered from the wings, wearing a *Cat in the Hat* hat and toting a book. She made her way to the foot of the stage, where a white rocking chair and floor lamp sat. She plopped in the chair, opened the book, and began reading. It was *The Lorax*. The students were enthralled. As she finished, Mrs. Roman, dressed as the Cat in the Hat, made a grand entrance and zigzagged through the gym, slapping students high fives.

Mr. Hay watched from off in the shadows, both happy and relieved. He still felt badly about any added pressure last year's assembly may have placed on the children. He might have been able to rationalize his tactics, had there been a positive impact on their scores, but that had not occurred. And so this time he had decided to ease up, to back off. Maybe, he said, today's performance would spur one child to head to the school library and check out a book. That would be reward enough.

The assembly was about over. It was time for Mrs. Schaefer to say a few, last words. Mr. Hay handed her the microphone. The mood in the gym shifted ever so slightly as she began to speak. Here comes one of her we're-all-in-this-together speeches, the students thought. A year earlier, the fourth and fifth graders recalled, she had practically begged them to take the exam as seriously as she. "I know it may not seem like your score matters, but every one of your scores counts," she had said, adding, "You have to say, 'The CMT is important to me, it's important to Brookside School.'" This time, though, there was no speech. Instead, Mrs. Schaefer led them in a cheer she had distributed on a handout sheet:

> *Brookside School is ready to take this test*
> *Brookside kids always try their best*
> *Brookside School is better than the rest*
> *Brookside School is the BEST!*
> *We can do it*
> *Yes we can!*

Perhaps because the children were tired, or because some thought the exercise silly, they said it with little verve. Mrs. Schaefer had them repeat it. The second time, they were louder. They still sounded, though, as if they were going through the motions, just to get the exercise over with. Last year she might have exhorted them to chant it again. This time she let it go. She returned the microphone to Mr. Hay. The children quietly exited the gym.

Representative Himes was running behind schedule. His aide told him he had just twenty minutes as he accompanied Mr. Morey and his students back to their classroom. Like the other VIP guests, he had been recruited to read to a class. Representative Himes was a big fan of Read Across America, and Dr. Seuss. His own two young children loved the Dr. Seuss stories. Mr. Morey closed the door to C-4, and the forty-four-year-old Democratic congressman dragged a chair to the front of the room. He sat down, opened a hard-bound copy of *The Cat in the Hat* and began to read. The students at the back tables moved to the rug, the better to hear. As he turned the pages, it was clear Representative Himes was enjoying himself. He grew increasingly animated, adding sound effects, reading lyrically. When he finished, he smiled and told the class how much it had been like reading to his own daughters, one of whom was in third grade, the other in sixth. "We live nine miles away, in Cos Cob," he said. He didn't mention how different his children's lives were from theirs. According to the 2010 census, the average Cos Cob home was valued at $969,100 and the median household income was $127,297. Nearly two-thirds of the adults twenty-five or older who lived there held at least a bachelor's degree. Of the community's 6,770 residents, 1 percent were black; 7 percent, Hispanic; and 86 percent, white. Just 3.1 percent lived below the poverty level.

The congressman shoved those thoughts aside; a few minutes remained before he had to leave. He gabbed with the students. "If you guys get together and decide you want a law for less homework, I'm the guy to talk to," he joked. "But I have to warn you, it's going to be real hard to convince me." While he spoke, Mr. Morey downloaded a photograph of the House chamber to his SMART Board. The congressman, taking his cue, reached for his wallet and pulled out what appeared to be a credit card. "This is what I use when I cast my vote on a bill," he said, explaining that he inserted the card into a scanner and pressed green for a yes vote and red for a no. "Any questions?" he asked.

Chandler raised his hand. "Have you ever met the president?"

"Yes, a couple of times, but just for a few minutes," Representative Himes replied. "He's a very busy man. He has to run the whole country."

The congressman's aide signaled him. It was time to leave. "I really enjoyed meeting all of you," he told the students. On his way out, he signed autographs for all who asked.

Two months later, sitting in his local Bridgeport district office, he ruminated on the gulf of opportunity that separated the Brookside kids from his daughters. "I'm conscious my girls have every advantage," he said. "They have two college-educated parents, at least one of whom is home to read with them and look over their homework. And they also get to go to great schools.

"Look," he continued, "it's a really painful thing for a guy like me who's in a position to help craft public policy, because the failure to well educate children has reverberations for the rest of that child's life. You do it right, and that kid becomes an engaged citizen and a productive member of a very powerful economy. You do it wrong, and that kid can end up as a ward of the state, one way or another, whether it's through incarceration or being economically unproductive. The stakes are so high on getting it right—or getting it wrong. I don't sit on the House [Committee on Education and Labor], but education is a very important issue to me."

And then, like so many parents, he tried to think of off-the-cuff solutions to some of Brookside's most pressing problems: For instance, why so few school parents turn out for Mrs. Schaefer's evening tutorials on how to improve their children's reading. "Look, it's a mistake to believe that parents aren't showing up because they don't want to," he said. "I've never met a parent who didn't fundamentally understand the importance of education. A lot of this is about urban poverty, a single mom with three kids who maybe works two or three jobs, or can't afford a baby-sitter." He paused. "What about childcare? What if you made childcare available to that single mom so maybe she could go to that PTA meeting or the teacher's conference?"

"Who's going to pay for it?" someone asked. "What's the likelihood of getting federal, state, or municipal funding?"

The congressman fell silent for a moment. He was an incurable optimist, he confessed. He acknowledged it wouldn't be coming from anywhere.

Mrs. Schaefer was quite certain Hydea would fail the reading and writing portions of the CMT. In fact, of the seven in her fifth-grade group, she felt confident in only three. No, strike that. She believed if Kevin, Carlos, and Jair, a student from Mrs. Bohrer's class, paid heed to every strategy she had taught them and conquered their own poor reading habits, they had a reasonable chance of passing. But, oh, Hydea.

A day earlier, Mrs. Schaefer had given the children their final, pre-CMT reading comprehension exam. The passage they were tested on, titled "A Trip to China," concerned a young girl who was traveling there for the first time, accompanied by her mother. The two planned to tour the Children's Palace in Shanghai, the Easter Pearl Museum, the Guangji Temple, and the Great Wall of

China. Most of all, though, the girl looked forward to seeing her grandmother, whom she had never met. Mrs. Schaefer's students had to read the passage, and then answer five multiple-choice questions and write two brief essays, all based on what they'd read. Hydea missed two of the multiple-choice questions. One asked, Where does this story probably take place? The first essay question asked, Which character in the story would you like to know, and why? Hydea chose the grandmother, but did not answer the second part of the question. The second essay question read, Using information in the story, write a paragraph that could have appeared in [the young girl's] journal. Hydea began her essay, "Today in China . . ." But in the passage, the girl had not yet traveled there. Mrs. Schaefer tried to guide her. "With this type of question," she said, "you're basically retelling the story. But it's a journal, so it's about feelings. Like, 'I can't wait to meet my grandma!'"

Hydea just didn't get it. Maybe it was the tension she felt as the exam drew nearer. Maybe it was the bad dream she'd had about failing the CMT, a dream she hadn't confessed to anyone at the time, not even her grandma. Or perhaps fifth-grade-level reading comprehension was simply out of her reach. Hydea felt terrible when she left the room, as lacking in confidence as she had ever been. Mrs. Schaefer, seeing how distressed she was, pulled her aside. "Hydea," she said, gently, "I know you have been trying your very, very best, and I can't ask any more than that." Hydea gave the tiniest of nods and shuffled down the hallway, toward her classroom. After she had disappeared around a corner, Mrs. Schaefer turned to one of the school volunteers who sometimes worked with Hydea, "She just bombed. Bombed. She just didn't get it at all. Based on today, she's not going to pass."

M r. Hay sat in his office scrolling through numbers Monday morning, the first day of the CMT. What he saw wasn't promising. "It wouldn't surprise me if we're back on that [failing list]," he said. "With the increase of proficiency requirements [to roughly 89 percent for a passing grade in language arts, 91 percent in math], it will make it very difficult for us to make 'safe harbor.' We probably have a tiny shot at getting it. We'd have to do ten percent better than last year, and that's a big jump."

One of Brookside's most troubling statistics, he said, was the low number of students who ranked beyond proficient, beyond goal—the category that corresponded to grade level, in Tirozzi's view—to qualify as advanced. The previous year, just 1.5 percent of the third graders, 3.3 percent of the fourth graders, and 8.3 percent of the fifth graders had achieved that level in reading, roughly the same numbers as 2003, the year he arrived at Brookside. He turned to his computer and opened a page that disaggregated the school's scores. "Look here," he said. "Our white children really didn't help us a great deal. We only had seven point five percent of them in the advanced group. There might be a school in the district that has thirty-five percent of their white students in the advanced group in reading. Our Hispanics and blacks are at two point nine and three point eight percent, respectively. And our economically disadvantaged is one point seven. That is telling me we still have a major issue there. We don't have enough kids reading at a high enough level. [Part of the problem is,] our kids with the ability to read at a high level are not being challenged enough, and they're not challenging themselves enough. An example might be, when they're taking a book out of the library or off the teacher's shelf, what do they pick? Do they pick a book that's pretty easy reading or one that puts a little challenge to them? Does the teacher monitor their selections closely enough?"

It frustrated him that he and Mrs. Schaefer had yet to find the key to boosting those numbers. He had had far more success with math. In 2003, just 3 percent of the students had qualified in math as advanced. By last year, those numbers had increased to 11.5 percent of the school's African American students, 27.5 of Hispanics, 50 percent of whites, and nearly 25 percent of those who were economically disadvantaged. Mr. Hay attributed these gains to a faculty that had come to believe in their students' potential. "When I came here," he said, "people had this mind-set that there was only so much [the students] could do. I'm a firm believer that if you teach kids at the lowest level, then guess what? That's what they will give you. But if you ask kids to do ten percent more, they'll give that extra ten percent. And that ten percent is very powerful." The secret, he said, is to find an achievable goal for children in the classroom. He gave an analogy. To an overweight person, he said, the challenge of losing fifty pounds appears overwhelming. But ask him to lose five pounds every few weeks, and suddenly it seems doable. "You have to convince your students to take those small steps," he said, "and when you do, you will find success—not with every student, but the majority will improve enough that they will jump up to that next level."

Mr. Hay swiveled back to his computer, searching for something, anything that might shed light on how to improve Brookside's reading scores. "If we can teach them math, we should be able to teach them reading," he said. "We know where we're weak—in nonfiction vocabulary, the DRP. We just have to find the key to teaching it, so that the kids get it. It's going to take longer. Reading is a tougher subject to learn than math."

Mr. Morey surveyed his class first thing Monday morning to see how they'd prepared for the exams. Hydea had gone to bed at nine the night before but had been so frazzled thinking about the test, she had left home without eating breakfast. Sergio had done the same. Marbella, on the other hand, had eaten heartily—eggs, corn muffins, milk. Breakfast was big in her family.

Mr. Morey checked the clock and strode to the front of the room. Fifteen minutes to go. He was anxious for the children, though he was careful to hide it. "The first test is editing and revising. Hydea, what are some of the things we can do to do our best?" he asked.

Hydea looked up, startled. She had not been paying attention. "One thing, Hydea, one strategy."

Hydea had never done well when put on the spot. She froze. Mr. Morey turned to her seatmate, Liz. "When you see something wrong, like spelling, you can underline it," Liz said.

"Yes, when you come across a mistake, mark it somehow," Mr. Morey repeated. He checked the clock again. It was nearly time. Quickly, he ticked off several other strategies: process of elimination, reading a passage to see if it sounds right. "There's one other thing to watch out for," he said. "There will be at least one sentence where no change is needed, where everything is already right."

A proctor entered the room; it was time to wrap things up. Across the hall, Mrs. Bohrer gathered her students in a wishing circle. Mr. Morey preferred to channel his inner basketball coach. "Boys and girls," he said, "we've practiced editing and revising fifty times, here and for homework. You've worked hard and it's going to show. You just have to try your best. That's all I can ask. It's time to focus now. Play time is over. You've got to buckle down and get it done. Don't do it for me. Don't do it for Brookside, or for Mom and Dad. Do it for yourself." He paused. "How does everyone feel? I feel good about this. How many of you feel confident?"

Five of the twenty-two raised their hands. *At least they're honest,* he thought. "Just do your best," Mr. Morey said.

Marbella wasn't happy. Math exams followed the editing and revising CMT. She didn't enjoy studying for them any more than she liked taking them. "They're very tiring," she told her mother. But her mother had laid down the law. Almost every night Marbella worked with her parents and sisters on math, which in some ways gave her more trouble than language arts. Division was her bugaboo, mainly because she did not know her times tables beyond five. To be perfectly honest, the fours gave her trouble, too. Given enough time, she could work out four times seven, but not seven times four. Many nights during the CMT, her mother had sat with her, trying to help her memorize her sixes, sevens, eights, and nines. But afterward Marbella hadn't practiced much. There was no reason to. She had figured a way around it.

That afternoon—the afternoon before one of the CMT math

exams—Mr. Morey had assigned fifty multiplication problems for homework. Marbella had taken the page of exercises up to her study and answered them all. "I did it by drawing lines on my paper," she said, and then demonstrated, writing down ||||| to represent five. She wasn't that worried about the coming test; she figured she could work out the problems on scrap paper, the same way.

In school the next morning, though, she wasn't so confident. "I started to worry when Mr. Morey handed out the test," she said. Afterward, she wasn't sure how well she did; the questions had been harder than she had anticipated. "I started falling asleep during the test. I, like, yawned and then I woke up again." Compared to math, she said, the language arts tests had been a breeze. For those, she had stayed alert the entire time.

Marbella hadn't been the only fifth grader who struggled to stay focused that morning on the math CMT. Ivette, one of the students in Mrs. Bohrer's class, was another who'd had other things on her mind. In the last two weeks, she had hardly spoken to her best friend, Carol. For quite some time, Carol had been smitten with Chris, one of their classmates, and now, unexpectedly, Ivette had fallen for him, too. Every day, it seemed, Carol penned notes to friends, asking if they thought Chris liked her. Obviously, it was an issue Ivette was reluctant to discuss. To complicate matters, Chris wasn't interested in either of them. He liked Kora, another of Mrs. Bohrer's students. When the class lined up to return from the cafeteria, he made sure to stand directly behind her. In gym class, he automatically picked Kora for his team. Unfortunately for Chris, Kora liked Kyle, from Mr. Morey's class. But that hadn't worked out, either. Kyle preferred horsing around with his buddies to paying attention to Kora. It was a vexing situation, all around. Ivette, a hardworking student, couldn't really approach Mrs. Bohrer with her problem. Somehow she would have to resolve this thing herself, and get back on track with her studies.

Week two of the CMT had begun. Fernando and Carlos sat at a computer in the back of Mr. Morey's classroom, working out the answers to a series of multiple-choice questions on earth science, magnetic fields, and electricity that Mr. Morey had found on the educational website Study Island. They were one of five two- and three-person teams seated at the classroom's computers. In fifteen minutes they'd switch places with five other teams, and return to their seats. The science portion of the CMT was approaching, and Mr. Morey thought the students might focus better working in pairs. "You're going to see questions like these, arranged in the same way, on the CMT," he told them. "I want you to talk each one through. I want you to work them out together."

To the students, it was a fun way to study. They jumped at any chance to leave their desks and work on the computers, and Study Island offered a welcome change of pace. Mr. Morey had pushed them hard the last week. Each morning, a CMT test. The rest of the day they studied for the next one, and the one after that. Like most of their classmates, Fernando and Carlos were exhausted.

The first question on the practice test dealt with how a river is born. "The answer's B," Carlos said.

"You sure?" Fernando asked.

"Trust me, it's B."

Carlos clicked "B" with his mouse. "Incorrect. Try again," the message on the monitor read. "No way," Carlos said. They needed the correct answer. The computer would not allow them to proceed to the next question till they answered this one right.

"It's C," said Fernando. He hadn't given the question any further thought, hadn't reread the multiple choices. He had picked it out of the air. Carlos clicked the mouse. Wrong again. Without waiting for Fernando, Carlos clicked "A." Same response. Finally, he selected D. "Correct!" the computer said. A new question popped up on the screen.

Beside them, Josh and Chris took their time and talked over each of the questions. So did Sergio and Monica. Sergio liked science, and he prevailed on his friend to think. It was like the four of them—Josh and Chris, Sergio, and Monica—were from a different classroom. The other two teams raced through the questions like Fernando and Carlos.

With eleven children at the computers and another eleven in their seats, reading their science text, Mr. Morey had a hard time monitoring all the action. He was a great believer in technology as a teaching tool—it was why Mr. Hay had given him the school's first SMART Board. But watching Fernando and Carlos, he wondered, What's the use? He called a halt to their work. "Boys and girls, the reason you like computers so much is because they give you instant feedback," he said. "But I sent you to the computers to give you an activity that would make you think. Clicking and clicking and clicking will get you the right answer. But getting the right answer like that isn't learning. I want you to take your time and talk over the possible answers."

The children returned to work. For a while they talked the questions through. But after a few minutes Mr. Morey heard the rapid clicking return. All year, he had tried to break them of that habit. How was he going to get through to them? He had encountered the same problem in the computer lab, whenever he had let them play an online math game designed to help them master their multiplication tables. They'd answer incorrectly and he'd hear *click, click, click*, always the same children, seeking a shortcut. *Maybe they'd stand a better chance on the CMT if they spent more time working out problems longhand,* he thought.

Josh, Mr. Morey's top student, had a secret he'd kept from everyone. Well, everyone except his best friend, Chris. The day before the CMT writing test, during recess, he told Chris he thought he might fail. "I'm not that good in writing," he confided. "The test is forty-five minutes, and I just can't write a lot without having to think for hours and hours."

Josh had worried about the writing exam since January 2, when CMT prep began. He'd grown ever more anxious, till in class on the first morning of the exams, he'd watched Mr. Morey approach with a test booklet and had turned nauseous. The writing portion, he knew, was just around the corner. He hadn't said a word to his parents, for fear of upsetting them. When he had unburdened himself to Chris, his friend had simply nodded. Chris lacked confidence, too. "That made me feel better, to know I wasn't the only one," Josh said. The two spent the rest of recess reminding each other of the test strategies Mr. Morey had taught them. Josh was certain he would panic and forget everything. "It's like, if you're alone in New York and you had to remember one person's phone number, I'd probably forget it because I was so worried," he said. He wished he knew what to do.

Hydea pursed her lips and opened her CMT science test booklet. She enjoyed science, liked doing experiments, but it wasn't her best subject. Just reading about the laws of sound or electricity in a book was confusing to her. She had to see a live demonstration to understand the concepts Mr. Morey wanted her to learn. This test was just words. She didn't feel too confident about it.

On top of that, she was hungry. Once again, she had been too nervous to eat that morning. Too bad Mr. Morey wasn't like Mrs. Bohrer, she thought. Mrs. Bohrer was famous for always passing out pre-CMT snacks. Hydea was unaware Mr. Hay had done the same when he was a teacher. Nor did she realize there was more to their act than simple human kindness.

"Back at my school in Massachusetts," Mr. Hay said, "we had lunch ladies with carts going mornings to the nine fourth-grade classes [before 2006, fourth was the only elementary grade tested under NCLB] with peanut butter bars and orange juice before the start of the test. If you've got a full belly, you can think better, and with the sugar in the bars, we were hoping they could stay more awake. We wanted them as sharp as possible, because there was so much pressure to succeed. We did the same thing my first two years at Brookside. We took money we collected from class photos and from magazine subscription sales and bought tons of those Pepperidge Farm Goldfish crackers from their day-old outlet store, and a beverage like Juicy Juice. Maybe they'll concentrate just a little better, I thought." He stopped when the third and fifth graders began taking the CMT, as well. With so many additional test takers, he could no longer afford the expense. But some teachers, he said, including Mrs. Bohrer, still purchased energy snacks for their students. "There's always things you can try, different things you can do to try to improve their scores," Mr. Hay said.

Though Hydea had been hungry on several of the test days, she didn't think it had undermined her scores. In fact, so far she thought she had done pretty well. "Every day when she came home," her grandma said, "I asked her, 'Well, how did you do?' And she'd say, 'Well, I think I did pretty good.' I asked, 'Was it hard?' And she'd say, 'Oh, no. But sometimes I ran out of time.'"

When Mrs. Schaefer learned that, her shoulders slumped. "It is what it is," she said. "All we can do is hope for the best."

Chapter 8

M r. Morey clapped his hands together, in that eager way men do when they're about to begin a new project. The CMT was over. For the first time in two weeks, his students didn't have to start school with a timed, pressure-filled exam, and then spend the remainder of the day preparing for the next one. After months of hard work, it would be easy, he knew, for them to relax and lose momentum. Eyeing the children, he could see them exhale, anxious to shift gears. But there were still three months left to the school year. He had to prepare them for middle school, and there was so much yet to do. Across the hall, Mrs. Bohrer threw an end-of-CMT celebration party. It was the day after St. Patrick's Day, and, after piling a table high with donuts, soda, chocolate chip cookies, chips, and chocolate chip cake, she demonstrated the Irish jig to her class. Mr. Morey chose a different tact. "Boys and girls, I have a question for you," he said. "What's a goal?"

"Something you set for yourself?" Jacky asked.

"That's right. How do you achieve that goal? Say, going to college."

"Study hard," Fernando said.

"Do your homework," added Kyle.

"The key to achieving a goal," Mr. Morey said, "is having a plan. Whatever your goal is, you have to decide, step by step, what you have to do to accomplish it. And then you have to follow those steps, each and every one. There are no shortcuts. Starting today, you're going to set a goal for yourself every week. It's for you and nobody else. It's going to be something you need to improve on. It can be an academic goal, like doing your thirty minutes of reading every night, which I know for a fact not all of you are doing. Or it can be a behavioral goal, like paying attention in class. I'm going to set a goal for myself, too—to be more patient. We all need to look at ourselves, to see what we can improve on." He circled the room, handing each student a sticky note. "I want you to write down your first week's goal and keep it on the top left corner of your desk," he said. "On Friday, we're going to see if you achieved your goal. We'll do this every week."

> Fernando wrote: Behave good
> Carlos: Behavior
> Sergio: Be more responsible
> Hydea: Pay more attention
> Chris: Focus more
> Chandler: Behavior

Leo: Read more

Marbella: Pay attention focus

At the end of the week, Mr. Morey surveyed the students. Some, like Fernando, hadn't given their goal a second thought. But the majority had done their best. Mr. Morey saw the difference—for that week, at least—in class. Hydea and Monica stayed focused. Chandler remained under control. Chris left his action figures in his desk. Mr. Morey wished he had thought this up sooner. Some of the students had actually begun to treat the goal-making like a game, a contest, to see how high they could achieve. It wouldn't last, he knew. They were children, ten and eleven years old. But for a day or two days or a week, perhaps they could glimpse their potential. For the next month, the child Mr. Morey was especially proud of was Fernando's friend Leo.

Mr. Morey liked Leo. Everyone in class did. He was a sweet, serious boy who was forever trying to guide Fernando toward better behavior. After Fernando had knocked the wind out of Marbella, it was Leo who approached him. "I told him this wasn't improving," he said. "I told him if he does something bad, then no one will become friends with him. I told him that he could be better at doing everything. I told him out at recess one day, I told him he could improve his homework and his schoolwork if he just tries. And if he does try, then everything in life will be easier. He said he would try to be better."

Sadly, Leo had troubles of his own. He was one of the poorest readers in the class, far too remedial to have been considered for Mrs. Schaefer's CMT prep group. He lived with his Ecuadorian parents; grandmother; and sixteen-year-old brother, Sebastian.

Though Leo's parents spoke English, they were uncertain how to help him. Early in April, at a parent-teacher conference, Leo's mother told Mr. Morey she was thinking of getting him a tutor. Mr. Morey knew they didn't have a lot of money; Leo's father worked as a manager at a local Gap, and his mother was a cafeteria worker at a nearby YMCA. "Why don't you just bring him here?" Mr. Morey suggested. "I'm here at eight thirty in the morning. Have him come in Tuesdays and Thursdays, and I'll work with him."

Their first day together, Mr. Morey had Leo read silently from *These Small Stones*, a book of poetry by Norma Farber and Myra Cohn Livingston, written for second to sixth graders. He wanted Leo to concentrate on decoding—sounding out words—from text simple enough that he wouldn't have to struggle with comprehension. He asked Leo to turn to a poem titled "Firefly: A Song."

"Ah, a song," Mr. Morey said. "What literacy device does that suggest?"

"Rhythm," Leo answered.

"Why don't you read it to me?" Mr. Morey asked. He led the boy to the front of the classroom and demonstrated how to hold the book high, just beneath his chin, so he could project with his voice. Leo read the poem robotically, like R2-D2, without inflexion.

Mr. Morey took the book from him and read it in a way that amplified its meaning. "We want to do more than just focus on reading words. We want to be able to understand the words," he explained. "When we understand the words, we become better readers. What is the firefly doing?"

"He's flying away," Leo said.

"What do you think the writer's doing? She's probably sitting in her backyard and she sees this tiny, bright light fly by, flying away. The author wrote it in rhyme for a reason. Why do you think?"

"So it's like seeing the firefly flying all over the place?" he asked.

"That's exactly right," Mr. Morey said. "Now try reading it again, and this time imagine it's you seeing the firefly."

Leo did slightly better, but ignored all punctuation.

"I want you to exaggerate the pauses a little bit," Mr. Morey said. "Do you know what that means? It means make the pauses a little longer."

Together, they kept at it for half an hour, the one reading, the other guiding, until Leo's classmates filed in. For a month, Leo made every early-morning session. He didn't make the progress Mr. Morey had hoped, but he did improve. In May, though, his attendance began to slip. Several times he showed up around 8:45 A.M., and then he simply stopped coming. Class field trips explained some of his absences, but not all. Maybe someone in the family had taken ill, Mr. Morey thought. Perhaps his parents' work hours changed. Or maybe Leo had lost the motivation to show up early week after week when improvement was so difficult to see. Mr. Morey never learned the answer.

Since February, Mrs. Madden, the school librarian, had been beside herself. The board of education members had announced at their monthly public meeting they would have to pare $5.1 million that spring to balance the 2011–12 school district budget. One member proposed they eliminate all twelve elementary school librarians, for a savings of roughly $600,000 in salary and benefits. It didn't take a genius, said Mrs. Madden, a high school graduate, to figure out why she and her colleagues had been targeted. None was a certified teacher, as the high school librarians were, so they weren't job protected. Worse still, they had no strong union to defend them. She sat, disconsolate, shaking her froth of short brown hair, facing a stack of books waiting to be shelved.

Mrs. Madden understood that in a budget crunch someone was bound to be squeezed. What she found maddening was the shortsightedness of it all. Didn't the board members see that this one-time savings would effectively cripple the twelve libraries? Who would order, purchase, catalog, and shelve books? Handle checkouts and returns? Run book sales to raise needed capital? Conduct reading programs for the three or four classes that visited the library each day? It struck Mrs. Madden that the board members didn't understand the role the library played in a Title I school such as Brookside—or how it differed not only from middle school and high school libraries but the community library, as well. At board meetings that spring, she and her colleagues tried to explain: Secondary-school students used the school library primarily for research—for term papers, special projects, and such. But the purpose of the elementary school library was simply to place a book in a child's hand. That wasn't as easy as it sounded. Take Fernando, for example. His parents couldn't afford to purchase books, and because they had no car, they had no way to transport Fernando to the public library. There were no newspapers, no magazines, no reading materials of any kind in his apartment, save a Bible. His parents were functionally illiterate in English, his father even in their native Spanish tongue. In his home, no culture of reading existed. Without the school library, Fernando would have few opportunities to discover a book, to take it home, to curl up with it, to develop a love and facility for reading. At Brookside, Mrs. Madden said, Fernando was hardly an exception. Even many of the better-off families had no book culture to speak of. As a result, she provided perhaps her most important function for Brookside's students: advising the children on what they should read. Mrs. Madden had made it her business to know every student's favorite genre. "Fernando likes to read comic books, *Ripley's Believe It or Not!*—the fun books with a lot of pictures," she said. "I don't think he enjoys reading. I think he likes looking at the pictures more, which is kind of sad. Hydea isn't a great reader. I don't think she enjoys it much, either. She pretty much gets what the other girls get, just to fit in. Marbella's the same. It's always that girlie-girl stuff, because it's easy, it's fun. Nonfiction is not a priority with her."

Mrs. Madden was so passionate about the library because she too had been raised in a home with few books. Growing up, she hadn't played school like Mrs. Walker or Mrs. Schaefer. "I was a horrible reader as a high school student," she said. "I told my own kids that. That's why I pushed the two of them to read, because I knew my lack of interest when I was younger played a role in my not going to college."

Mrs. Madden landed her first job at Brookside in 1994, working in a first-grade classroom as a teacher's aide. Her daughter, then a fourth grader, had transferred to the school the year before. Mrs. Madden is one of those people who seem perpetually in motion, and soon she was spending her down-time in the library, helping the librarian catalog and shelve books. By familiarizing herself with children's literature, she thought, she could better help her own kids' learning. Mrs. Madden found she loved the sight of a child—any child—transported by literature. On her own, she studied the Dewey Decimal System, mastered the art of repairing cracked bindings, learned the nuances of leveled reading. Twice she applied for Brookside's librarian position, though she lacked a library science degree. The second time, she was hired.

Mrs. Madden immersed herself in her job. She initiated a reading club for preschoolers aged three and four. She enabled students to check out three or four books at a time, where before they had been limited to one. She taught them the Dewey Decimal System, so they could find titles on their own. She worked sixty-hour weeks (while being paid for thirty-two) preparing for her big fund-raisers, the school's semiannual, book sales. With Mr. Hay's support, she modernized and expanded the library collection. "A new book would get me so excited," she said. "I would take it home at night, and I couldn't wait to come back and tell the kids, 'Read this one, it's really good.' I would put a sign on one of the tables: Mrs. Madden's Picks of the Week." Many days, she spent more time at the library than at home. Her love for the room, for all it represented, was plain to see. "A child will say to me, 'Do you have such-and-such a book?' and I'll say, 'Go over to that shelf and look under this number and it's a blue cover.' 'How do you know that, Mrs. Madden?' she'll ask. It's because I touch the books every day. Eleven years is a long time to be touching books," she said.

And now the library seemed in jeopardy. In mid-April the board floated a new proposal: It would retain all twelve librarians, but cut their weekly hours from thirty-two to nineteen. Nineteen was key. It placed the librarians one hour below full-time status, meaning they would forfeit their pension and benefits, including healthcare. A month later, in mid-May, after some push back, the board revised its plan. Dr. Marks, the new school superintendent, proposed that the board eliminate half the librarians, with each of the remaining six covering two schools. Mrs. Madden had worked eighteen years for the district, but only eleven in her current position. At least six other librarians were more senior than she. In another month, it appeared possible she would be out of a job. She sought out Mr. Hay.

Mr. Hay was sympathetic. By nature, he wasn't touchy-feely, but Mrs. Madden knew his concern for her and, especially, the library. He had spearheaded the building of a library in one of his Massachusetts schools, and after he left it was named in his honor. He believed strongly that the library was the hub of an elementary school, its most important room. He tried to reassure Mrs. Madden. But in fact, he had little influence over the school district's budget. And the library wasn't his only financial headache. Recently, the board had proposed another cost-cutting move: eliminating the assistant principals at several schools, among them, potentially, Dr. Masone. It was also possible Mrs. Schaefer's position would be downsized. On top of that, for the last month the flag outside the school had flown perpetually at half-mast. The lanyard on the flagpole had broken, and Mr. Hay did not have in his budget the $3,000 it would cost to fix it. Earlier that spring, the school had won $10,000 in a contest sponsored by a local online newspaper, and had raised another $8,000 at its annual auction night and banquet. (A similar fund-raising event in wealthy, neighboring Westport or Darien, Mr. Hay noted, might generate

$50,000.) But that money had already been ticketed for new $7,000 risers to replace the school's old, rickety ones and to upgrade classroom electronics equipment.

"Be patient," he told Mrs. Madden. "Nothing's been decided yet." His words brought her little solace. She returned to the library, sat at her desk, and let her eyes drift round the room.

Mr. Morey had an idea. The curriculum schedule called for him to teach the Constitution, and he thought, *Why not have the students act out the legislative process?* He had never tried such a thing before. The next day in class, he explained, in a simplified manner, the path a bill must follow before it is signed into law. "Your homework tonight," Mr. Morey said, "is to come up with five bills you'd like to see this class adopt as law." The next day he picked the two best, rewrote them and distributed copies to the students. He titled the first bill, Professional Fridays. It read:

Students will dress "professionally" every Friday for the rest of the school year. In business, many companies have a "casual Friday" where workers get to dress in a more relaxed style. Since just about every day in school is casual dress day, it is proposed that students dress professionally once a week.

Boys (including Mr. Morey) will wear dress pants, a button-down or collared shirt, and a tie (optional).

Girls will wear a skirt (below the knee), dress pants and blouse, or a dress (below the knee).

Boys and girls will have to wear dress shoes. If it is a gym day, sneakers can be brought in.

If there is a special event on a particular Friday, then the class will decide if the Professional Friday can be canceled for that day.

The second bill, titled Healthy Snack, read:

Students will bring in only healthy snacks for lunch and special occasions. We live in a society where there are many people developing health problems because of the foods they eat. These health problems not only hurt people's bodies, they also hurt people's checkbooks. People spend thousands of dollars every year paying for medical bills and health insurance. We could save a lot of money by eating healthier and paying lower medical bills.

Only healthy snacks will be brought in during snack time.

Only healthy snacks will be brought in for celebrations like birthdays or parties.

The class will create a "menu" that has healthy alternatives to unhealthy snacks.

Water and juices will be substituted for drinks high in sugar and sodium like sports drinks, sodas and fruit drinks (fruit punch, Kool-Aid, etc.)

The students' enthusiasm surprised him. By acclamation, they elected Jacky president. Mr. Morey assigned twelve of the other eighteen students present that day to the House, and the remaining six to the Senate. He then named Marbella, Aajah, Monica, and Brie to the House committee in charge of the Healthy Snacks bill, and Hydea, Carlos, and another boy to the Senate committee that would hold hearings on the Professional Fridays bill. "You are the legislators," Mr. Morey told them. He stepped aside, returning to his desk. "I thought they would pass one [Professional Fridays] and veto the other, never bringing it to a vote, and we'd move on to the next lesson," he said.

Instead, the students took their legislative duties seriously. After some debate, both bills passed out of committee, then passed out of the full House and Senate, only to have the Senate committee reject the House's Healthy Snack bill and the House committee do the same with the Senate's Professional Fridays bill.

Mr. Morey watched with amazement as Marbella, the self-appointed head of the House committee, suddenly took charge. Applying her persuasive skills as adeptly as President Lyndon Johnson might have, cajoling this committee member, arm-twisting that one, she muscled a rewritten Professional Fridays bill first through the committee and then the full House. Out went the dress shoes requirement on gym days, in went leggings with skirts as appropriate dress wear for girls. House Leader Marbella and her colleagues sent the revised bill back to the Senate committee and then the full Senate, where it passed 6–0. The president immediately signed it into law. Marbella celebrated, slapping high fives with her fellow legislators. The Healthy Snack bill eventually passed, too, with amendments of its own. Mr. Morey couldn't get over Marbella's accomplishment. "I know this is weird coming from a teacher," he said. "Choosing a social life over education is a big no-no. But there's a part of me that thinks, this is an important quality to have. Marbella isn't a natural student, but one way or another, she's going to be okay. She'll find a way to be productive in life." As far as he was concerned, it was the best school day Marbella had ever had.

Mrs. Schaefer shut the door to her office and sat beside a first-grade boy whose reading was already below grade level, and whose progress had stalled. They were at the table where last year she worked with Matthew. "Say the word, *and*," she said. The boy repeated the word. "Now write it on the board," she directed, handing him an easel the size of an iPad. She had him point to each letter in succession and then pronounce the word again. She did the same with the word *the*. Mrs. Schaefer then handed him a picture book titled *Looking Down*.

"What is the first thing you do?" Mrs. Schaefer asked.

"I take a picture walk," the boy said. Together they turned the pages. As they did, the boy described the action he saw.

"Now what do we do?" Mrs. Schaefer asked, when they reached the end.

"Now I go back and read," he said.

The boy stumbled on the first sentence: "He is riding a bike." The boy interpreted it as: "Here is my bike." He stopped, confused, knowing something was wrong. His words did not match up with the picture of a boy pedaling his bicycle. Mrs. Schaefer placed the easel on the table and wrote in large letters, *he*. Beside it, she wrote, *she*. She had the boy point to the letters she had written. She combined them into words, and said the words aloud. "Now you," she said, pointing to the easel. He did so and then returned to the book. He reread the sentence. Now it made sense. The boy turned the page.

It was mid-April, and Mrs. Schaefer still hadn't had a chance to read with Matthew. She had been swamped with weekly, grade-by-grade planning meetings with faculty over what to teach and how, with in-class demonstration sessions on Reading and Writing Project workshop teaching techniques, and with struggling, emerging first-grade readers. Matthew still missed her, still stopped her in the hallway when they passed, still asked when they could read together again. It always saddened Mrs. Schaefer to hear him, but in fact, she knew Matthew had more reading support than most. Mrs. Walker, his teacher, was particularly skilled in teaching the subject, and Mrs. Schaefer had trained Mrs. Carbo, Mrs. Walker's classroom aide, in the workshop technique, as well.

On this morning, while Mrs. Walker read *Miss Rumphius*, a grade-two-level book by Barbara Cooney, to the rest of the class, Mrs. Carbo read *Mr. Putter and Tabby Bake the Cake*, a picture book by Cynthia Rylant designed for a first- or second-grade audience, with Matthew. "I really want you to help me," Matthew told her. "I will," Mrs. Carbo said, "but it's important that first you try on your own."

Matthew had read the book before. He had read several in the twenty-book series about the everyday-life adventures of a grandfatherly man and his elderly cat. This one was about the Christmas cake Mr. Putter decided to bake for his neighbor Mrs. Teaberry. Matthew's affinity for the books came naturally. For years he'd had his own pet cat, Cuddles.

The very first sentence—"It was wintertime."—gave Matthew trouble. Mrs. Carbo told him to point to *wintertime*, the word on which he had stumbled. "Do you see a word inside there that you know?" she asked. Matthew did. "In," he said. It was enough of a hint to clue him to the word, and to the meaning of the sentence. He read through the first of the book's four brief chapters with little problem, but the second chapter proved difficult—the punctuation threw him—and the last two chapters challenged him even more. Like an out-of-shape runner, Matthew lacked stamina—largely because the books he insisted on reading at home were beyond his reading level, making it hard for him to get through them. It had caused considerable frustration for Mrs. Schaefer, who had discussed the issue repeatedly with Matthew's parents, and now with Mrs. Walker and Mrs. Carbo it was doing the same.

When he finished reading, Mrs. Carbo asked him to retell the story. Matthew did so, flawlessly. His verbal skills were fine. "Now I want you to write down what you just told me," she said. A new set of problems arose. First, Matthew asked to go to the bathroom. Then he wanted to tell Mrs. Carbo a story he remembered from another book. When it came to the tale about Mr. Putter and Tabby's cake, he needed a push, it seemed, to write one word, and then a next. After ten minutes, Matthew had managed just two sentences. Apparently, he lacked the confidence to translate his thoughts to paper. This was nothing new. In class, he fell further behind. Mrs. Walker reported his continuing problems to Mrs. Schaefer. Upon hearing them, the literacy specialist was disappointed, but not surprised. *Maybe I'll model a workshop lesson for the second-grade teachers in his classroom and look in on him,* she thought. But Mrs. Walker was the most skilled of the second-grade teachers, and Mrs. Schaefer had already scheduled a workshop session with Mrs. Canal's second graders, and Mrs. Sweeters, another second-grade teacher, had asked if she could be next. *I'm only one person*, Mrs. Schaefer reminded herself.

Mr. Morey's classroom door was shut and the room dark when Fernando arrived in class one early May afternoon. He cracked open the door and peeked inside. Mr. Morey was showing some kind of educational film. The boy made a big, noisy production of getting to his seat. His classmates tried to ignore him.

Fernando had spent the previous forty-five minutes with his mentor, a sixty-one-year-old man from nearby Stamford who had volunteered to work with him as part of a school district–sponsored program designed to help the community's neediest and most troubled kids. Fernando had been with his mentor for nearly two years, with few tangible results. He continued to pick on classmates, even those he called friends, and often disrupted class. The mentor spoke with him continually about his quick temper, which led him to spur-of-the-moment bad behavioral decisions— elbowing Marbella to the ground, for instance, or acting the fool in class. His mother admitted to school administrators she had little control over him at home. Still, the mentor remained hopeful of turning him around. "If you just count to ten before you act, you'll make the right choice," he told the boy. But Fernando never counted to ten. He rarely counted to one. As Leo had warned, he had already lost friends. During recess, few classmates sought him out on the playground. Sergio, who lived across the street, seldom played with him anymore; Sergio's older brother had made his disapproval of Fernando clear.

Fernando plopped down at his desk in the front of the room, beside Mr. Morey, where the teacher could keep an eye on him. He fumbled for a notebook and a pencil. On the SMART Board was a Discovery Education program about the life cycle of a plant. Fernando had missed half of it. He didn't know where to begin.

"You need help?" Carlos asked.

Mr. Morey looked up. Carlos was often thoughtful of others, but this was particularly generous of him, he thought. The two boys had once been close, but had drifted apart. Maybe after all this time, Mr. Morey thought, something had finally clicked with Carlos. Maybe he was beginning to mature. That was more than Mr. Morey could say for Fernando, who ignored Carlos's offer and acted up almost immediately. On the screen, an insect landed on the trigger hairs of a Venus flycatcher. Instantly, its leaves slammed shut. "Hah, hah! You're trapped, you're trapped!" Fernando cackled, pointing at the SMART Board

"Quit it," Chandler ordered. "Why don't you be quiet?" added Carlos. Mr. Morey watched, but didn't say a word. Discipline from a classmate carried far more weight than any message he could deliver. Fernando immediately fell silent, and the class went back to watching the film.

Mr. Morey didn't know it, but his words from a few months earlier—"I don't feel like teaching you anymore," after Chandler and Carlos had acted out for the millionth time—had affected the two boys deeply. For all the trouble they had given him, they sincerely liked Mr. Morey. In fact, he was their all-time favorite teacher. "Because he's a man and he plays football with us outside, and he's fun, and he shows me what to do, and right from wrong," Carlos said. "I was dancing in my house when my mom told me last summer I had him," said Chandler. After Mr. Morey's troubling remark, the two had talked. It was time, they had decided, to shape up. Even after that, they weren't perfect, as Chandler was the first to admit. There was the day, he recalled, when Mr. Morey had unloaded on the class—the two of them in particular—for misbehaving yet again with a substitute teacher. Mr. Morey had threatened to recommend that they repeat fifth grade the following year—only not in his class. "You're not mature enough for middle school," he had said. Once again, they felt they had let Mr. Morey down. If only they could live up to his expectations, they thought. It would be like making their own fathers proud. Both knew they had done the right thing in hushing Fernando. Neither had sought Mr. Morey's thanks. They didn't have to. For once, they could read the approval in his eyes.

Mr. Hay opened the *Norwalk Hour*, the local newspaper. In it, on an inside page, was a photograph of Brookside students performing in the school's spring musical, *Seussical Jr.* The caption said there would be three weekend performances, staged in the gymnasium. Not the greatest plug he had ever seen—no story, no mention of the cast of thirty-seven students, or the 125 hours of rehearsal they had put in, nothing of the costumes Mrs. Kline, one of the preschool teachers, had created, or special-effects black lights the director, Mr. Beckley, a third-grade teacher, had employed. Still, it was helpful publicity that strengthened Brookside's community image.

It was certainly more beneficial than the school's recent appearances in the media. Several weeks earlier, the Reverend Al Sharpton had arrived on campus, accompanied by a made-for-television crowd of protesters. A Bridgeport woman had illegally enrolled her child at Brookside, without paying a hefty, out-of-district fee. Norwalk had decided to prosecute her, to discourage other nonresidents from doing the same. It was unclear to Mr. Hay what the Reverend Sharpton was protesting, or why. All he knew was Sharpton had timed his appearance to coincide with the broadcast of the local evening news. Several months earlier, the NBC-TV *Today Show* news anchor and co-host Natalie Morales had visited Brookside to tape a segment for a documentary on the relationship between nutrition and how students perform academically. She identified the school, but not the city where it is located.

It could have been worse, Mr. Hay thought. At least neither Sharpton nor Morales had faulted Brookside for anything. It had been several years since a parent had come to him, saying she was transferring her child to another Norwalk elementary school.

The school year was drawing to a close. One by one, while their classmates read silently at their desks, Mr. Morey called a series of students—his slower readers—to an isolated table in the front of the room. Hydea's turn was coming. She could feel it. This would be her last big test of the year, in some ways her most important one—the Developmental Reading Assessment (DRA2), the standardized test that would determine her reading level as she exited fifth grade. Already, she was sweating it. To reach grade level, she would have to read a 230-word long fiction or nonfiction passage in no more than two minutes six seconds, making no more than eight mistakes, while exhibiting proper expression and phrasing, and then pass a writing comprehension test based on what she had read.

Minutes earlier, Marbella had taken the test. Hydea had sneaked a peek at her as she had taken a seat beside Mr. Morey. Marbella had seemed nervous. That wasn't surprising. Like Hydea, she had started the year reading at a low fourth-grade level. After she had dropped out of the afterschool reading program, expectations for her hadn't been high. Marbella opened the booklet Mr. Morey handed her and began reading. She seemed to be doing okay, but she spoke so softly, Hydea couldn't tell. When she finished, Mr. Morey administered the comprehension test. That was a good sign. One had to pass the reading exam to advance to the comprehension segment. Hydea hoped she'd make it that far. She had begun the year reading with the fluidity and accuracy of a fourth-grade student, but with a third grader's comprehension skills. Recently, though, she had been surprising herself. The other day in class, Mr. Morey had read them a Robert Frost poem, "The Road Not Taken," and Hydea had raised her hand. She had been doing that more frequently. "I think the two roads are about making a choice," she had said, and Mr. Morey had told her, "That's a great thought." All those hours with Mrs. Schaefer, she decided, must have helped her ability to focus and to think. At home and in class, she now spent a lot more time actually reading, instead of soldiering through a page or two and then losing her concentration. She certainly felt more confident, and some of it had carried over to her private life as well.

Hydea was going through another of her bumpy patches with Marbella and Aajah. A few days earlier on the phone, she had gotten into an argument with Aajah. As always, the subject had been Marbella. During lunch that day, Aajah and Marbella had spent a lot of time talking and giggling among themselves, even with Hydea seated beside them. Hydea had complained to Aajah, her best friend, that she was feeling left out. Aajah hadn't really known what to say; often so animated, she had fallen silent. After hanging up the phone, Hydea had sat her grandma down. "I need some advice on friendship," she had said. Her grandma had a sense of what had been going on between the three girls. "She told me, 'It's all right not to have close friends in school. You're there to learn,'" Hydea recalled. "I was kind of happy that she said that. The next day I just did my schoolwork. Aajah came up to me and apologized. I told her I forgave her, but I know she likes Marbella better than me now. I still feel close to both of them even when things happen, because I trust them. But I know something's going to change if we have more arguments." Earlier in the year, she acknowledged, she wouldn't have handled being shut out so well. It was a real show of maturity, her grandma believed, her first step toward independence.

Mr. Morey interrupted her thoughts. "Hydea," he called, waving her to the table. "I was real nervous," she said. Her passage was a fictional piece about a man with supernatural powers who used them for nefarious means. "He was traveling, and he stayed at a friend's house and he was not a very good person," Hydea said. Mr. Morey directed her to read. When she finished, she looked up. He handed her a booklet with space for four short essays. Hydea was pleased with herself. But she had advanced this far before. One question gave her trouble. "You had to summarize what the whole thing was about," she said. "The problem was trying to figure out how I should start it and how to explain it." First, she said, she tried to picture the story in her head, like Mrs. Schaefer had suggested. It didn't work; she had been so focused on reading quickly and clearly, she couldn't recall much of the story. So she reread it, penciling a check mark beside each key detail, again as Mrs. Schaefer had taught, and then composed her summary. But when she read it over, it didn't make sense. "I didn't explain the words correctly," she said. "So I tried going back to the story, and I took the details that I understood most and put them in, and it made sense." When time ran out and Mr. Morey collected her booklet, she was uncertain how she'd done. Back home, she told her grandma, "I'm not sure I got it right."

When Mr. Morey sat down to grade the girls' exams, he wasn't confident, either. He started with Marbella. Her test had been a nonfiction passage on gray wolves. He had already been impressed by how confidently she had read, finishing the 230-word article in one minute and forty-eight seconds, while making just two mistakes. Her speed placed her at midrange for a fifth-grade reader, and her accuracy ranked as advanced.

He turned to her writing segment. The main question she had to answer was this: What is the key to a gray wolf's survival? Marbella wrote, "I think the most important thing about gray wolves is that gray wolves always stay in packs.'"

"That's dead-on," Mr. Morey said. "That's the most important thing. And then you want to see why she would think that. She wrote, 'I think this is important because it's easy to catch a deer or elk. I also think this because it's easier to hunt for animals if you're in a pack.' That's dead-on, too. She was really thinking about it. This is a big change for her." Clearly, something had clicked for Marbella. *Maybe it was the cheating episode,* Mr. Morey thought. Ever since, he said, she had been far more diligent about her schoolwork. But it was impossible to know for sure. With children, he said, there could be a dozen motivating factors, many of which he might not be aware of or even be able to guess. That had turned out to be the case with Marbella. Mr. Morey had no idea Marbella's mother had put the fear of God into her before the CMT: Do better or risk repeating fifth grade.

Mr. Morey turned to Hydea's exam. Her situation was different. Mr. Morey and Mrs. Schaefer had always agreed Marbella had the potential to reach grade level that year in language arts. That hadn't been the case with Hydea. Sure, she could decode words. But what use was that if she could not find in them meaning? Mr. Morey expected to find the written equivalent of radio static—a collection of stray sentences jumbled together in a way that made little sense. But she had nailed her essays, almost as effectively as Marbella had. "I looked hard at her work, because I didn't want to just give her [a passing grade]," Mr. Morey said. "But it was legit." He recorded Hydea's score and set down his blue marking pen. "I was looking at her work and got tears in my eyes, it was so cool," he said. The test the two girls had passed certified them both as average fifth-grade readers.

Epilogue

M r. Hay, dressed in short sleeves, was in his office idly scrolling through lists of test results on his computer screen, relaxed, taking his time. The school was all but empty. It was a hot,
humid midmorning in July. Earlier that month, he and his wife
had traveled to coastal Oregon to attend their younger daughter's
wedding. For very different reasons, this was another day he'd
been awaiting. The state had posted the 2011 CMT scores. He
had just begun to review them when Mrs. Schaefer strolled in,
dressed casually in a blouse and Capris. Mrs. Schaefer, having finally given her notice, was now retired. Several weeks earlier, the
school had thrown an elaborate party for her and two other retiring teachers at a country club on the shores of Long Island Sound.
But her heart was still invested in the students she'd coached, and
she didn't mince words. "How'd we do?" she asked Mr. Hay.

There was good news and bad news, he said, and launched into the bad news first: Brookside was still failing. In fact, by NCLB standards, its situation had grown worse. The school had lost its "safe harbor" designation—not only had it failed to make "adequate yearly progress," it had failed to improve its overall score by "safe harbor's" required 10 percent. Mr. Hay didn't mention that a second, equally poor showing in 2012 would result in Brookside being categorized as a school "in need of improvement." Potentially, that could trigger a wide range of consequences: from interventions in the form of administrator and faculty retraining, to mass firings, including Mr. Hay and the teaching staff, to the state department of education taking over the school (though the last two options were extremely unlikely). Only 67.1 percent of the students had reached proficiency in reading, and a total of roughly 89 percent was needed. The school had come much closer in math, he told Mrs. Schaefer, with 88.9 percent achieving proficiency, about 2 percent short of the target number. Whites were the only demographic group to pass either subject.

The good news, he said, was that Brookside slowly but surely was raising the curve. In the last five years, since 2006, the staff had lifted an increasing number of students from "below basic"—remedial level—to "basic" or even "proficient," and had boosted a like number from "proficient" and "goal" to "advanced." Mr. Hay showed Mrs. Schaefer the fifth-grade comparisons over that period.

READING SCORES

YEAR	BELOW BASIC	ADVANCED
2006	26.4 percent	13.9 percent
2011	17.5 percent	15.9 percent

WRITING SCORES

YEAR	BELOW BASIC	ADVANCED
2006	6.9 percent	13.9 percent
2011	0 percent	22.7 percent

MATH SCORES

YEAR	BELOW BASIC	ADVANCED
2006	12.5 percent	16.7 percent
2011	0 percent	29.7 percent

The improvements seemed to buoy Mr. Hay more than they did Mrs. Schaefer. "I'm not so fixated on our CMT scores," he told her. His main concern was moving students forward—"up the ladder," in his vernacular—from "below basic" to "basic," from "basic" to "proficient," from "proficient" to "goal," from "goal" to "advanced." Mr. Hay had a mantra: "They call you a failure when you know you're not," he told anyone who asked. "Parents, politicians—they grew up thinking sixty percent was [passing]. We have almost nine out of ten passing here, but they say we're failing. *I* know we're doing the right thing." He had implanted this in the school years before, to raise staff morale. For the most part, it had worked.

Take Mrs. Bohrer. "Everyone talks about our CMT scores," she told her nonteacher friends, "but no one gives us credit for taking a slow fifth-grade reader and lifting him two grade levels, if he's still [failing]." Of course, she was right. Given the challenges Brookside's teachers faced—the impoverished students, the school parents nonconversant in written and/or spoken English, the students whose dreams seldom extended beyond the local community college—there had to be some goal that kept them going. Otherwise, sooner or later they would be forced to ask themselves: What's the point?

It would take nearly another year, till May 2012, for the U.S. Department of Education to offer Brookside administrators and teachers hope for relief from the school's failing test scores. Seven years after then–state Commissioner of Education Betty Sternberg sued the U.S. Department of Education for a waiver from No Child Left Behind regulations and lost, U.S. Secretary of Education Arne Duncan approved a revised state educational reform plan and named Connecticut the eighth state (as of July 2012, there were thirty-two, plus the District of Columbia, with applications pending from five additional states) granted flexibility in implementing its own education reforms. Connecticut's waiver application emphasized three main objectives: to boost high school standards to ensure that graduates were college or career ready, to provide increased professional training and support to teachers and principals, and to hold its poorest-performing schools more accountable. But there was a fourth element to the plan. Henceforth, the progress of a school's struggling students—the overlooked achievers cited by Mr. Hay and Mrs. Bohrer—would factor into whether a school passed or failed.

On this July 2011 morning, though, Mr. Hay's interpretation of the scores brought Mrs. Schaefer little solace. "I can't say I'm surprised," she said, resignedly, upon learning the school had fared so poorly. She changed the subject, asking Mr. Hay about his daughter's wedding. The principal clicked on a photo album he had already uploaded to his computer. Soon enough, though, conversation returned to the reading scores. Mrs. Schaefer had devoted almost the entire year to training teachers how to implement the Reading and Writing Project workshop model, and nine weeks to coaching her handpicked CMT prep groups. None of it had worked as well as she had hoped. She didn't like leaving an untidy mess. Mr. Hay sensed something was troubling her.

"I've been retired now for two weeks," she told him. "I'm just not comfortable with it. I think I might have made a mistake."

It was too late to be undone. *Un*retiring in the Norwalk Public Schools system is a complicated process, once paperwork has been filed. In any event, budgetary issues had since intervened. Mr. Hay had lost the money necessary to fully fund her old position. He had already negotiated to hire Mrs. Schaefer's former colleague, Mrs. Balsinger, to replace her on a part-time basis. "Part-time," Mr. Hay said, disconsolately. "We're a failing school, we do poorest in language arts, and we're down to a part-time literacy specialist." He told Mrs. Schaefer he'd like to hire her on a consulting basis—if he could find the funds.

Money informed almost every major decision that shaped Norwalk's public schools that summer and over the following school year. For Mr. Hay, the most immediate was the matter of Brookside's school library. Quietly, he had lobbied behind the scenes, trying to preserve Mrs. Madden's job. "I told them [at the district office], it's critical to keep the library open. If a child's taking out five, six, seven, eight books a week, as some of them are, and we now have the library open only every other week, that means there's a week they don't get those eight books. Multiply that by twenty [weeks—half the school year]. That's one hundred sixty books they don't get to read. I told them, you become a good reader by reading.

It's practice. For many of these kids, this is the only library they can get to. It's going to impact us dramatically in the long run if we don't have an opportunity to get books in their hands."

In the end, following a contentious budget hearing, the board restored the elementary school librarians' full-time jobs. They imposed their cuts elsewhere, mostly on the district office staff. Among those let go were the district's grant writer, head literacy specialist, and director of elementary school education. "The grant writer!" Mr. Hay said, upon hearing the news. "That's the last person I would have cut. This district needs money. If the grant writer's doing his job, he brings in anywhere from two to ten times his salary." Dr. Marks, the new superintendent, said relatively little throughout that critical meeting. Asked later how she could permit the board to eliminate the district's chief literacy specialist, given the district's failing scores on the language arts CMT, she glumly replied, "Apparently, I didn't make a good argument for it. I take responsibility." It was her first budget negotiation. She appeared overwhelmed.

Mr. Hay got rid of his Hummer, purchased a Hyundai. Outside of that, little in his life changed during the following 2011–12 school year. He continued to live in the austerely furnished apartment he rented from Mrs. Magrath. Weekends, he commuted to Massachusetts to be with his wife. That left him plenty of quiet time—in his office, his apartment, during his three-and-a-half-hour weekly drive home and then back—to mull the situation at Brookside. He had three years (he had decided to work an additional year) till his planned retirement. He searched for a new program to champion before he left.

Early in the school year, he escorted Barbara Dalio, of the Dalio Family Foundation, headquartered in the neighboring, wealthy town of Westport, Connecticut, on a tour of Brookside. The foundation, Dalio said, was interested in helping fund public education. Perhaps they could help with textbooks. Mr. Hay proposed a different idea. "I read a study," he said, "that children who grow up without a home library of at least twenty books tend to be less successful in school than those who do." Over the years, he explained, he had rewarded students with books: for improved grades, perfect attendance, good behavior, for any number of things. It was his stealth strategy for getting kids to read. Not long after, the foundation presented the school with a $10,790 check. Mr. Hay went shopping at Scholastic and purchased five books apiece—two fiction, three nonfiction—for each of Brookside's roughly five hundred students, for every kindergartner through fifth grader in the school. "Imagine," Mr. Hay said. "Every kid now has their own home library. If we're lucky, some of them will fall in love with reading. They'll be different students after that." For many, he knew, these were the first books outside the Bible that they—and perhaps their parents—had owned.

It was to be one of the few worry-free moments of his year. He no longer had a full-time literacy specialist. In January, he lost Dr. Masone, the assistant principal, for the remainder of the school year; she took an extended leave to care for her new baby daughter. He held little hope his students would score well enough on the 2012 CMT to save Brookside from failing a second consecutive year and being designated a school "in need of improvement." And on the horizon loomed a $9.9 million proposed budget cut that would trim Brookside's 2012–13 resources to the bone. Mr. Hay believed that such a cut could cost the school system anywhere from forty to eighty jobs. Mrs. Madden was once again in jeopardy. So were Dr. Masone, Mrs. Balsinger, the Academically Talented teacher, the string instruments teacher, the $10,000 in new books and services Mr. Hay had intended for the library—maybe more. "Ten million dollars," he said. "That's the equivalent of closing two of [Norwalk's] nineteen schools."

Mr. Hay clasped his hands, placed them in front of him on his desk. "Sometimes I look at job openings—not that I'm going anywhere," he said, "and I'll say, what kind of school is that? I'll click onto [a state department of education schools database] and say, hmm, they have two hundred fifty kids—two hundred forty-five who are white, two Hispanics, and three blacks—and they're running ninety-six percent on the CMT. And I'm going, hmm, I wonder what *that* life would be like. I've always said, our teachers in this building do such a great job of taking their clay and molding it and getting success. It's different when kids are coming with everything. Basically, they do well, they score high. But I always wonder, if their teachers didn't show up, would those kids still score high? Our teachers have to show up."

A fter the dust settled from the June 2011 budget crisis, Mr. Hay found money to rehire Mrs. Schaefer as a part-time literacy consultant. Once a month, she conducted Reading and

Writing Project workshop training sessions for the teachers and helped with their curriculum planning. Every six days, she trained Mrs. Carbo and the other teachers' aides in the same workshop techniques. In addition, she worked numerous hours helping slow readers. It amounted to a comfortable schedule—four hours a day, three days a week. She was able to travel to Italy for three weeks, spend a winter week in Florida, and, most important, visit three days a month with her new granddaughter in Pennsylvania. She had never been so unhappy. "I missed my professional life more than I thought I would," she said. "It was frustrating, especially at the beginning, walking into the school and not being able to do what I used to do—be the main literacy specialist."

She grew more comfortable as the year progressed. The teachers still consulted her, still came to her for advice. She made peace with her reduced role. Together with Mrs. Balsinger, she organized a new set of CMT prep groups and worked hard with the students—as hard as she'd worked with Hydea—though just twice a week. Eventually, Mrs. Schaefer approached Mr. Hay. She hoped they could work out a similar arrangement for the following school year, she said. Mr. Hay was all for it.

Then in early May 2012, five weeks before the school term ended, he asked if they could talk. The budget crisis had flared. With district finances in disarray, he said, he would soon run out of money to pay her. He cut her workload to three hours per week for the remainder of the school year. It remained unclear whether he'd be able to hire her the following fall. Mrs. Schaefer feared she'd have to abandon her professional life a second time, probably for good. She was torn. She had retired from Brookside primarily to devote time to her granddaughter. But a part of her wished she had never left.

Midway through the summer after their fifth grade graduation from Brookside, Hydea received an unexpected call from Marbella inviting her to a trampoline party. Hydea was excited to go. Her grandma escorted her across the busy street. For much of the afternoon, she frolicked in Marbella's backyard. Aajah wasn't there. She was away somewhere, Marbella said. There were four or five other girls at the party. Some Hydea knew, others she didn't. But they all had a wonderful time together. The afternoon flew by, and before Hydea knew it, it was time to head home.

It was the last time she and Marbella would play together outside of school. Hydea didn't visit Aajah that summer, either. That fall, in middle school, Hydea made a new group of friends. At lunch, she sat with them at a large table near the cafeteria door. Marbella and Aajah sat with their own group, three tables away.

At first Hydea thought she'd be unhappy apart from her old pals, especially Aajah. But she found herself caught up in a whole new social dynamic. She liked middle school. She spread her wings a little, as she'd begun to do at Brookside. Her fifth-grade CMT scores hadn't been great—"proficient" (passing) in reading, "basic" (below grade level) in math and writing, "below basic" in science—but they were better than she had ever managed before. And there had been no words to describe her pride on learning she had reached grade level that year in reading. She was struck speechless when Mr. Morey had told her the news and slapped her a high five. To herself she had thought, *I'm where I should be! Whooo! Yes! Finally!* In middle school, she continued to work hard, and one semester made the honor roll. She hoped, as a seventh grader, to follow her sister Billi onto the school basketball team.

Marbella had surprised all her teachers at Brookside with her CMT scores: "goal" (above average) in both reading and writing, "proficient" in math, "below basic" in science. Mr. Morey and Mrs. Schaefer believed she had turned a corner. So did her parents—especially when, one middle school semester, she made high honors. The teachers, she said, had caught her attention; they were far more demanding than her elementary school teachers, even Mr. Morey.

Socially, Marbella's life had changed, as well. Though she sat with Aajah at lunch each day, they weren't the inseparable pair they'd been at Brookside. She'd drawn closer to one of her oldest friends from elementary school, a girl who'd been in Mrs. Keefe's class. There wasn't any reason Marbella could point to that would explain the change in her friendship with Aajah. It might have been as simple as two growing girls and a summer spent apart. "I don't hear them talking much on the phone anymore," Marbella's mother confirmed. She added that Marbella was reading more.

Upon hearing her mother's words, Marbella felt compelled to offer a clarification. "It's not because I want to," Marbella insisted. "It was assigned." She had read some books—she couldn't remember their titles—to meet her independent reading requirement. The stories were okay, she admitted. They went down quickly, perhaps because at home, tucked away in her alcove, she had fewer distractions. She no longer had Bieber fever. The singer's pictures were gone from her school locker. He was so fifth grade.

A number of Mr. Morey's students had blossomed at middle school—a school, it should be noted, that until the 2010–11 school year, like Brookside, had been failing. Josh, Kyle, Chris, and Carlos had all been named Citizen of the Month. So had Kevin, from Mrs. Bohrer's class and Mrs. Schaefer's CMT prep group. Chandler and Carlos had both calmed down and had buckled down in the classroom as well, Carlos making the honor roll and Chandler earning high honors. But not all his former students had succeeded. Fernando was in trouble constantly, picking fights, bullying others, not doing his schoolwork. He was disciplined numerous times, both with in-school and out-of-school suspensions. His guidance counselor had arranged for Fernando to see a therapist at no charge to his parents, but his mother—perhaps because she had no car—had never followed through. Near the end of fifth grade, Fernando had written in an assignment for his ESL class that he was thinking of eventually joining a street gang, "but just part of the time." That had triggered a meeting with Officer Holmes, the school's DARE officer, who explained there was no such thing as a part-time gang member. Fernando dropped the subject, though he wasn't sure he believed the policeman. Mr. Hay, upon learning how often Fernando had been in trouble in middle school, worried that there would come a day when the boy would fall to a gang's sales pitch. "Fernando's a follower," the principal said. "He probably doesn't get a lot of attention at home. The gangs will let him know they want him, and he'll want their approval." He thought it such a shame. Despite all, Fernando possessed real potential. Though in reading he had scored "basic" on the CMT, in science he had ranked as "proficient" and in math and writing he had achieved "goal."

M r. Morey mused about his old class throughout the summer. A situation would arise—maybe he'd see two kids horsing around outside the movie theater and he'd think, oh, they remind me of Carlos and Chandler. But the first day of the 2011–12 school year, he pushed thoughts of that group aside. He had twenty-five new students to focus on, three more than the previous year. So many, that he didn't have enough desks for them all. Two would have to sit alongside one another at what had been a computer table for the entire school year.

The additional students made teaching difficult. Where he used to pull three or four children out for small-group instruction, he now grabbed eight or nine. One-on-one time was much rarer than before. He had a high number of slow readers and too many immature boys, making his work harder still. He didn't teach the civics lesson that had worked so wonderfully with Marbella, Jacky, and the rest—"the best lesson I ever taught in my life," he said—because he feared his current class wouldn't take it seriously enough, and he didn't want to risk its memory being tarnished.

His greatest challenge, though, was teaching math. Math was his specialty; he was a member of the district's math steering committee. The district had adopted a new textbook series, called Go Math!, that was more closely aligned to the state's new, planned curriculum, which was scheduled for implementation in 2014. Connecticut had joined a consortium of forty-five other states, plus the District of Columbia (as well as the U.S. Virgin Islands, the Northern Mariana Islands, and Guam) in adopting what was called the Common Core State Standards Initiative, its purpose being to coordinate national standards in language arts and math. The district had offered Go Math! to the twelve elementary schools in 2011–12 as a pilot program. Six schools, including Brookside had adopted it. (The other six Norwalk elementary schools chose to remain with their existing texts, meaning in the district that year, three separate elementary school math programs were taught and that the following year, math teachers at the city's four middle schools would somehow have to herd all their students onto the same page.) Mr. Hay, always the innovator, wanted his faculty to get a leg up on teaching the new program. The switch proved difficult at first, for both teachers and students. One day during a frustrating lesson, Mr. Morcy found himself referencing Hydea. "I had a student last year who struggled a lot," he told his new class, as they wrestled with an algebra lesson and seemed on the verge of giving up. "But she worked really hard, and by the end of the year she had made tremendous progress, more than she could have imagined. You guys can do it, too, if you work hard, like she did."

Mr. Morey hadn't thought of Hydea in a while, hadn't seen her since the last day of school the previous June. That had been a memorable afternoon. The children had cleaned their desks, packed their things. Class was just a half day, and they had been eager to leave. While the girls exchanged good-bye-for-summer hugs and the boys slapped hands, Mr. Morey had struggled with how to say his own good-bye. Just before dismissal, he had asked for quiet. He told them how proud he was of the progress they'd made. He urged them to make good choices in life. "If you ever need anything, I'll be here for you," he told them. Softly, he added, "I'm going to miss you guys. I love you guys. Good luck." He then had walked to the doorway, and exchanged hugs and hand slaps with each student as they left his room for the final time. When Aajah reached him, she had started to cry. He had had to turn away to keep from doing the same.

"Teachers aren't supposed to hug kids," Mr. Morey had said later, back in his classroom, after the last school bus had gone. The school district, he explained, wanted them to avoid any appearance of impropriety. "But how can you not?" he asked. "People who talk like that haven't been in a classroom. They don't know what goes on. It's different for a fifth-grade teacher than for teachers in the lower grades. Next August, they'll see their kids in the hallway. But our kids leave the building. Some of them will come back to visit, but it's not the same."

Acknowledgments

This book began, as with every good thing in my life, with my wife, Carol. I'd been toying with the idea of examining life in a struggling elementary school when Carol—who has been Brookside's speech pathologist since 2001—suggested I serve as a volunteer in the school's student-mentoring program. "I think you'll love it," she said. I did. Thus began a long-term relationship with Brookside's students, teachers, and administrators that led me in the spring of 2010 to approach David Hay, the principal, with a proposal: In return for the daily, unfettered access I would need to research this book, including to classrooms, curriculum-planning sessions, literacy workshops, and CMT-prep training, I would serve as an unpaid teacher's aide. Because Mr. Hay is a risk taker, because we had come to know one another through my work with several of his troubled students, and because he was curious to learn an outsider's perception of his school, he agreed.

I settled on Brookside's fifth graders because they were older and generally better able than the younger students to express their hopes, triumphs, frustrations, and feelings. I chose Marbella and Hydea because of their complex relationship, both academically and socially. I selected Keith Morey because by reputation I knew him to be one of the school's most open and inventive teachers and because his class included the two girls. Linda Schaefer was an easy choice; as Brookside's literacy specialist, she was at the heart of the school's quest to pass the CMT.

In some ways, an elementary school classroom is like a cabin at a summer sleep-away camp. When the door closes, it becomes its own insular world. Friendships blossom and wither, triumphs and tragedies play out, leaders are born. Seated day after day in my own school-issue, molded chair, on the opposite side of the room from Mr. Morey, beside the pod of students nearest the door, I had an unvarnished view of it all. Adults forget, these many years later, what it is to share a room with twenty-two fifth graders, not all of whom are simultaneously eager to learn. I sure had. When it all works, as it did with Mr. Morey's civics lesson, the teaching process is exhilarating. But far more often, it requires a degree of patience and love and tolerance and firmness that far exceeds what I possess.

To Mr. Morey's students—all of whom I observed and many of whom, with their parents' or guardians' permission, I interviewed—I give my grateful thanks. Hydea, Marbella, Josh, Sergio, Chandler, Aajah, Monica, Liz, Jacky, Leo, Chris, Sara, Kyle, Brie, and all their classmates—I am indebted to each of you, for your willingness to accept me as the twenty-third member of your class. It was a pleasure to share Mr. Morey's room with you each day and to come to know you all.

One teacher does not describe a school, and I spent time in several classrooms, including those of Jeanette Keefe, Linda Walker, Jeri Magrath, Jennifer Sweeters, Dorothy Brown, and Alison Prunotto. Over the course of the school year I also interviewed Jenna Masone, Alma Samuel, Bonnie Lindsay, Fawnia Henneghan, Jeff Beckley, Karen Canal, Shannon Roman, Susan Gilroy, Tracey Sutton, Adele Bernstein,

Hector Rivera, and Tim Downey. To a person, they were generous with their time and insightful in their thoughts about their profession and their students. (In the manuscript, I changed one teacher's name; like the four children whose names I disguised, she did not play a main role.)

Aside from Mr. Morey, the teacher I owe the greatest thanks is Annette Bohrer. I spent parts of nearly every day in her fifth-grade classroom, across the hall from Mr. Morey. It was through observing her that I gained perspective on the teaching process and saw how simple kindness and caring can encourage learning in a way that no textbook can. I owe equal thanks to her students—Zayda, Kevin, Carol, Chris, Jasmine, Edwin, Kora, Jair, Ivette, and all their classmates—for accepting me as their classmate as well.

I want to give thanks, too, to the others who so generously granted me interviews: Susan Marks; Gerald Tirozzi; Peter Behuniak; Doug Rindone; U.S. Representative Jim Himes; Paula Madden; Ralph Sloan; Sandra Morey; Charlie Bohrer; Matthew and his mother, Kathleen, and brother, Daniel; Sergio's brother, Odelis Jr., sister, Alejandra, and father, Odelis; Edwin's mother, Gloria; Audra Good; Bill Israel; Holly Balsinger; Salvatore Corda; Steve Leinwand; Craig Creller; Steven Colarossi; and Janet Steinberg.

To Mr. Hay, Mr. Morey, and Mrs. Schaefer; to Marbella and her parents, Maria and Mario, and sisters, Melanie and Maryrose; to Hydea and her grandmother Josephine, I will never be able to offer proper thanks. They opened their lives to me when they had no obligation to. Every author should have such lovely and generous people as their subjects. I wish nothing but the best for them all.

My wife, Carol; my brother, Randy Berler; and his wife, Linda Berler, were kind enough to read each chapter as I finished, and offer advice and encouragement.

I owe an enormous debt to my editor, Andie Avila, who championed this book when it was nothing but a proposal and who edited my manuscript with care and thought. Throughout, she showed enormous trust, which I hope I have rewarded.

I have known my agent, Alice Martell, since college. She is calm and wise and encouraging and witty, and throughout this two-year project was forever in my corner, there to protect me—especially on those days I wanted to go ten rounds with myself. She was the first to encourage me to write this book and then went ahead and sold it, forcing me to actually follow through.

Last, I would like to thank my mother, Ruth Berler, who taught fourth grade for more than twenty years at Norwalk's Wolfpit Elementary School, five miles from Brookside. Because of her, school—and what, at its best, it can be—is never far from my mind.